ENHANCED

It's Not Enough to Just Believe

Nathan Neighbour

Sermon To Book
www.sermontobook.com

Enhanced: It's Not Enough to Just Believe / Nathan Neighbour
ISBN-13: 978-1-945793-89-9

Nathan Neighbour is one of my favorite forces for good in the world. His wisdom is only matched by his deep desire to see people thrive and step into a life fully enhanced. I have personally benefited from his leadership. And now with this book you can, too.

Jason Jaggard
Executive Coach, Speaker, and Founder of Novus Global

For anyone who's ever had a challenge connecting the dots between believing and living the reality of the Scripture, this book is for you. Nathan artfully examines ways to supplement our faith, step by step, in practical ways. He offers each one of us an opportunity to step into our world afresh and enhance our experience of love with God and others.

Jean-Marie Jobs
Founder and President of GAP Community

Nathan has a rich heritage of previous authors in the Neighbour family. His great-great grandfather penned over 300 books, his great-grandfather over 12, his grandfather over 40. But this book, the first of many, shows a contemporary writer speaking powerfully into his generation. Every chapter will stimulate your desire to mature in Christ. Read it with a highlighter in your hand. I did!

Dr. Ralph W. Neighbour Jr.
Best-Selling Author, Speaker, and Global Cell Church Consultant

To my sons, Jackson Brave and Collin Blaze:

May you risk for love and live with passion.

Choose life.

Always, Dad

Acknowledgments

Thank you to my wife, Marla, who is the clearest representation of Christ in my life. You see me, and still you choose me over and over again. Your love and support are my lifeline.

Thank you to my parents and grandparents. My continuing legacy of faith, love, and hope and my commitment to serving the greatest movement on the planet exist because of your prayers (and at times, sweat and tears). I hope I become half the giants that you are.

To Jean-Marie Jobs and our GAP Community team: Your investment in my life and our world has inspired me to live by faith and take far greater risks than my small human eyes see to be possible.

Finally, to Humanity Church: Thank you for allowing me to lead with you, play harder with you, go further with you, create so much beauty with you, and dream so much bigger with you than I could on my own. You are the greatest version of Jesus to our world that I can imagine.

CONTENTS

INTRODUCTION

Finding Your Divine Nature

What is faith?

Some people claim that faith is a cop-out, a way to avoid wrestling with the questions at hand or to avoid dealing with the struggles of life. Those who believe in God are often called "people of faith," as if those who choose to not put their faith in a higher power somehow aren't people of faith. The reality is, everyone has faith in something. Statistics show that in California, about nine people are killed each day in traffic accidents.[1] Despite this fact, thousands of Angelinos are still confident enough to get in their cars and drive to work each morning. They have faith that they will reach their destinations safely.

Going to the doctor requires faith in your physician, that they'll make the right diagnosis and prescribe the right treatment. Even eating at a restaurant requires some faith that the food will be properly handled and prepared and safe to eat.

It's not that we need *more* faith, but we need to simply

shift our faith to something that works—something trustworthy that actually gets us the results we're longing for. Humans were obviously designed to have faith in something. The question is, is our faith moving us toward the life and future we long to create?

Have you ever put your faith into something or someone that wasn't faithful? A bad investment? That guaranteed job opportunity? A used car salesman? You'd never fall for that twice. Yet, how often do we keep returning to put our faith into people and things that consistently leave us empty? We must stop trying to do things on our own and blaming the past, others, or circumstances for our place in life. Instead, we need to seek out the path that will transform our faith into reality.

Hebrews 11:1 defines faith as *"confidence in what we hope for and assurance about what we do not see."* Our lives become tangible evidence that what is unseen is real. We are those who translate the invisible into the visible.

But what kind of faith do we need to have to see the results promised us? Do you ever feel like God is playing a game with your life? He tells us we only need a tiny seed of faith to move mountains. Yet, many of us don't see mountains moving in our lives on a regular basis, if ever. If the amount of faith isn't the issue, what gives?

When my wife, Marla, and I were planning our honeymoon, we decided on a seven-night stay in an all-inclusive resort in Cancun. All the food, drinks, entertainment and excursions we could handle were ours for one romantic and luxurious week. I'll never forget driving up to our tropical paradise, getting out of our van, and immediately being offered a cold drink in the hot, humid lobby entrance. I accepted; Marla declined.

After checking in and getting our resort wristbands that act as an all-access pass, we were about to head to our room when Marla stopped me and said, "You forgot to pay for your drink!" I paused, laughed, and explained to her that all-inclusive meant everything is free—it was all paid for in our reservation. She instantly flagged down the attendant for her "free" drink.

In 2 Peter 1, the Scriptures let us in on this this powerful spiritual reality:

> *His divine power has given us everything we need for a godly life through our knowledge of him who called us by his own glory and goodness. Through these he has given us his very great and precious promises, so that through them you may participate in the divine nature, having escaped the corruption in the world caused by evil desires.*
>
> ***—2 Peter 1:3–4***

What if God had set up the game of life in your favor? He tells us that we have been given everything we need for the powerful life of faith that we were made for. You've been granted a spiritual all-access wristband to a life filled with the awe and wonder that comes with engaging in a relationship with Jesus, complete with all its rights and privileges. From this new vantage point, scarcity and playing small should never be an option when it comes to our faith.

You may be reading this and thinking, "I've heard all this before," and you probably have. This is a part of the dilemma. There's a world of difference between being granted access to something and actually accessing it. There's a chasm between knowing and fully embodying that knowledge.

Had Marla and I been unaware of the access given to us with our resort wristbands, we would have still had a good honeymoon. However, we would have missed out on the abundance that was available to us at any moment on our trip. We would have spent unnecessary money, time, and energy on that which was already ours.

Some of you have not yet fully stepped into the reality that God has already given you everything you need for the Godlike life you were called to live. "Already given" means it's available—not one day, not when you finally get your life together, not when you mature—but here, in this present moment, you have everything you need for this life. It's Jesus' divine gift to all who follow Him.

I find that most people are uncomfortable with the word *Godlike*. To be honest, when it first came out of my mouth, it sounded incredibly heretical. Christians are often much more comfortable with the terms *Christlike* and *godly*. However, if we believe that Jesus was fully divine, then those words are synonymous with *Godlike*. If you are made by God and for God, it would make sense that He would call you to a Godlike life. To choose anything else is to choose a lesser life.

However, just believing a Godlike life is available isn't enough. For many of us, our faith is more informed by Disney than the Scriptures: we believe that when we wish upon a star, all our wildest dreams will come true. This fantastical version of faith can never be realized and will always leave us disappointed in the end.

If you choose never to access this God-given gift, you'll still live a decent life, but will miss out on the abundance that is already yours at any moment. You will spend your money, time, and energy on living an average and manageable existence. However, no one dreams to have it said of them that they lived an average life at the end of their days.

Living with authentic faith requires that you first recognize you've been given everything you need to live a Godlike life, and then acting on that knowledge. Once you are willing to do that, the trajectory of your life will shift from a corrupt state to your divine nature.

The Divine Nature

We were made by and for God, and we carry His divine spiritual DNA within us. However, we are naturally drawn to rebelling against and resist submitting to Him. Only when we submit to God can His power flow through us, transforming every part of our being. It requires way more faith to believe that humans are flawless than to believe that there is a spiritual brokenness within us. If you look at the state of humanity, it isn't hard to see this internal darkness leaking out in many forms, such as racism, abuse, war, arrogance, and human trafficking.

This internal state of rebelling against our God-given image is often referred to as sin and will constantly move our lives toward corruption and destruction. Our default desires for our own control and power keep us in this perpetual state of spiritual breakdown.

However, if we are willing to release that need for

more control and power and partner with God, then there is space for Him to work in us, and through us. We must let go of our need to be God, so that we can become like God. Our divine nature that was placed within us from the beginning can then finally start to work its way out and into our faith. Right now, we can only dimly see this divine nature that lives within and around us, but as we allow God to work, it becomes much clearer.

We're all familiar with the cartoon image of a little devil and little angel standing on a cartoon character's shoulders, attempting to win them over to their side as the character makes decisions. This simple image might not be too far from reality. We are in the process either of being moved toward corruption that comes from our own internal desires or of participating with God in moving us to our divine image.

This whole journey of faith can be summed up as a fight to keep participating in that divine nature and achieving it here and now. We aim to remove anything and everything that is corrupting our spirits, so that we can once again return to the Godlike lives we were designed to live.

Peter continues with his insight on this journey:

> *For this very reason, make every effort to add to your faith goodness; and to goodness, knowledge; and to knowledge, self-control; and to self-control, perseverance; and to perseverance, godliness; and to godliness, mutual affection; and to mutual affection, love. For if you possess these qualities in increasing measure, they will keep you from being ineffective and unproductive in your knowledge of our Lord Jesus Christ. But whoever does not have them is nearsighted and blind, forgetting that they have been cleansed*

from their past sins.

—2 Peter 1:5–9

Just as vitamins and probiotics help your body to become stronger and improve your physical health, enhancing your faith with these spiritual supplements will strengthen and fortify your spirit for the long haul. They will prevent your knowledge of God from becoming ineffective and limiting your experience of who God is and what He can do.

This list of supplements isn't random either. There is a clear order:

Supplement faith with goodness.

Supplement goodness with knowledge.

Supplement knowledge with self-control.

Supplement self-control with perseverance.

Supplement perseverance with godliness.

Supplement godliness with mutual affection.

Supplement mutual affection with love.

Each one builds upon the other and creates a clear path that we all must engage if we are committed to living in our divine nature. For example, the knowledge of God is pointless if you don't first believe that He is good. Self-control is worthless without the knowledge of what exactly to control. There's nothing to persevere through if you never start controlling yourself—and so on.

You certainly don't have to take this journey, but you

can't get away from putting your faith in something.

You also can't get away from supplementing your faith, constantly adding elements that will fortify it. The people or things you put your faith in and what you add to that faith both reveal and refine your character. All of this affects your destination in this life and your perception of God.

When we choose to not engage in a faith journey with Jesus, we find ourselves frantically putting our faith in anything and everything that seems to get us close to the life we long for. They may feel right in the moment or create a sense of control amidst the chaos, but, in the end, they leave us empty.

- Some of you have faith that you can do this life on your own. This faith is supplemented with struggling to prove yourself and being overworked, unhealthily driven, and resentful. Its destination is burnout, exhaustion, and bitterness. You miss out on experiencing how God transforms weakness into power.
- Some of you have faith in your dysfunction, illness, or disease. This faith is supplemented with fear, anger, and pride. Its destination is hopelessness and lethargy, and you miss out on experiencing God as your Healer and Redeemer.
- Some of you have a strong faith that life has handed you the wrong cards and you are powerless to make any changes. This faith is

supplemented by victimization, reliving the past, bitterness, and emotional shutdown, and its destination is spiritual death. You miss out on experiencing how much God is for you.

- Some of you have faith that your past defines your future. This faith is supplemented by apathy, frustration, impatience, and resignation, and its destination is stagnation. You miss out on experiencing how God creates beauty out of our chaos.

When we put our faith into those things that move us toward corruption, our thoughts become spiritually unproductive and ineffective. In other words, the things of God that we know to be true lose their power to transform us and others. We also lose our spiritual sight—we can't see what's right in front of us and we forget where we've been. We start to wonder if God really is who He says He is.

Over the course of this book, we will look at each of these enhancements in depth: goodness, knowledge, self-control, perseverance, godliness, mutual affection, and love—one at a time. It's designed to be a trail guide for the journey of enhanced faith.

We often fail to live the full, abundant life Jesus has promised, not because it isn't available to us, but because we forget who we are in Christ. We are the chosen ones and heirs to the kingdom of faith, love, and hope. Our shortcomings have been forgiven, and we are set free to move mountains and illuminate the dark places of this world.

We are called by God into the most dynamic life we could ever live—an adventure called faith. It all starts with a decision to go on the quest for our divine nature by supplementing our faith.

Will you take this journey?

CHAPTER ONE

Goodness: It's All Good

I work with a non-profit, GAP Community, that trains people around the world in leadership and transformation. One aspect of our youth training involves the teens participating in a high ropes course. It's powerful to see these young people developing their willingness to trust and take risks with others, but I'm nervous around extreme heights.

I know these rope courses have been safely and expertly built. In fact, the ropes can hold the weight of a small airplane! But every time I get out there, I am very intentional about shifting my perspective from anxiety to excitement, from the possibility of failure to the possibility of adventure. Instead of focusing on fear and worrying that the ropes might break, I remind myself I am completely safe and can trust those ropes.

Goodness—the first enhancement for our faith—is likewise an issue of perspective. Unless you're crazy, you will never put your trust in something or someone you perceive as broken, wrong, or bad.

Many people lose their faith in God—or refuse to put their trust in Him—because they can't reconcile how a good God can allow bad things to happen. I don't blame them. Who would want to follow a God who leaves tragedy in His wake?

When we find ourselves in circumstances that are not good, we often try to convince ourselves otherwise. "It's all good" has become the common cultural motto we use when talking about our own difficult situations, even though we know it isn't. Christians often respond to other people talking about their life tragedies with kneejerk cliché phrases like, "Well, God is still good," even though their circumstances don't seem to reflect that truth.

Looking at our lives, we see pain, suffering, disappointment, and betrayal. Looking at the world around us, we see violence, injustice, corruption, prejudice, and greed. Faith in a good God can seem like a risky proposition. Who would be interested in that type of goodness?

On the other hand, it is quite easy to put our faith in something we perceive as good, trustworthy, and beautiful. If you're sitting down while reading this, you didn't think twice about the faith you're putting in your chair. It instantly appeared trustworthy and good from your vantage point.

It's all about seeing things from a new perspective. The person who anticipates the ropes course as an exciting adventure would feel as if the designers specially designed it for someone like them. They would see this masterpiece as good.

The Essence of an Artist

Humanity Church is in the heart of the arts colony in downtown Pomona, CA. I live among and work with world-class artists on a weekly basis. Whether I'm observing a film maker, poet, or master painter, I love watching artists at work, taking the invisible and making it visible for us. Artists create from the depths of what is inside of them. They have an amazing ability to convey great joy and hope—also the pain and suffering of the human experience.

You can look at artists' works and tell what was happening internally for them while they created. Likewise, an artist cannot create something that is contrary to what lives inside them, as that would be contrary to who they are. Artists create from their essence.[2]

In the same way that artists put forth what is inside them, God poured Himself out when He created the earth. In fact, the first image of God that Scripture presents to us is that of an artist: *"In the beginning God created the heavens and the earth"* (Genesis 1:1). He, too, created from His essence:

> *Now the earth was formless and empty, darkness was over*

> *the surface of the deep, and the Spirit of God was hovering over the waters.*
>
> *And God said, "Let there be light," and there was light. God saw that the light was good, and he separated it from the darkness.*
>
> ***—Genesis 1:2–4***

He spoke creation into existence, taking that which was invisible and making it visible. Everything that He created is good, including humanity: *"God saw all that he had made, and it was very good. And there was evening, and there was morning—the sixth day"* (Genesis 1:31).

Goodness is part of God's essence, for all things that are good are produced from love, and God is love Himself. God created a good environment that was fueled by His love. God poured His love into creation.

Love cannot produce anything other than goodness; therefore, neither can God. However, for love and goodness to exist, the choice of freedom must also exist.

The Goodness of Freedom

One morning, my young son, Jackson, was inconsolable. Having tried everything else, I offered to make him one of his favorite meals: waffles. I spent a good half hour preparing them—I even added fresh blueberries. But once the waffles were ready and we sat down together for what I hoped would be a father–son bonding time, he refused to engage with me, screaming, "No, Mama!"

I tried forcing him to stay at the table with me, I tried hugging him, I tried persuading him, but everything I tried to make Jackson love me seemed to push him further away. It was a frustrating and fruitless experience for both of us. I was not Jackson's choice to love at that moment, and there was nothing I could do about it.

The object of our love must have a choice to stay or walk away; otherwise, it's not love but coercion.

We all want *our* freedom until someone uses *their* freedom to hurt us, to betray us, or to inflict pain on humanity. Then we want God to intervene and remove choice from the equation. People often question the goodness of God due to the suffering we see around us. Most human suffering is the result of people abusing their freedom. However, you can have freedom (and with it, love) or you can have control. You can't have both.

In the beginning of humanity, God gave Adam and Eve everything, including that choice to love and obey Him freely.

> *And the LORD God commanded the man, "You are free to eat from any tree in the garden; but you must not eat from the tree of the knowledge of good and evil, for when you eat from it you will certainly die."*
>
> ***—Genesis 2:16–17***

The tree of the knowledge of good and evil in the Garden of Eden was not some random morality test for Adam and Eve. They already had the knowledge of good. In fact, all they had known was good. God wanted to protect them from knowing evil.

So, why even put the tree in the garden? If God had not given them the option of choosing to reject His love by defying His command, their love would not have been genuine. By giving them a choice, He could know that their love for Him was genuine. God is interested in relationship, not in coercion.

This reveals the heart of God for humanity. To say that God isn't for us is simply a lie. He set up the world in our favor, attempting to keep us from the knowledge of evil, so that we could enjoy a perfect relationship with Him and live out our purpose of love. Does that not sound like a good God? It feels like a divine setup, for goodness sake.

Unfortunately, the story didn't end well for Adam and Eve. Because God loved them and wanted their love, He gave them a choice. The serpent tempted Eve to eat from the tree. She did, and she invited Adam to join her. As a result, their eyes were opened. For the first time, they knew evil and lost their innocence and purity. And death entered the human story.

The Consequences of Freedom

Adam and Eve had lived in an environment with an endless number of good, life-giving choices and only one choice that would lead to death. They could have engaged in extreme sports and potential danger with little consequence. They could have gone swimming with piranhas or taken naps with tigers with no ill effects. They were in the protective bubble of God's dominion. Today, we take our lives in our hands simply by leaving the house!

Adam and Eve's freedom to eat from the tree led to death. To this day, every human being is repulsed by the reality of death. I've never officiated a funeral where those attending were completely at peace with the death of a loved one. This is an echo of our origins; we were not designed to die. Goodness was meant to live on forever. But with humanity now marked by evil, evil might live on forever as well.

Death was the consequence of disobedience, but it also shortened the life of evil. If humans now had a physical expiration date, so did the evil they performed. Can you imagine the chaos, the oppression, the hopelessness, if violent criminals and power-hungry dictators lived forever on earth? What would the world look like if sex traffickers could abuse their victims for all eternity? Death became a stopgap for evil, though it would not be the end for humanity.

The masterpiece of creation had been corrupted. If we had been in God's position, we would have been overwhelmed with anger, frustration, and feelings of betrayal. At the very least, we would've wiped the canvas clean and started over.

But because God is good, He responded with love, compassion, and patience. He made suitable clothing for Adam and Eve to help protect them in their vulnerable newly fallen state. God did not abandon them.

In fact, the story of Scripture could be summed up as a good God pursuing a humanity that is committed to choosing less than the goodness in which it was designed to live. The gift of Jesus became the path for us to return to Eden, alleviating us from the mark of evil and returning us to goodness, purity, and power.

It Starts with Perception

Because we don't fully understand God's goodness and compassion toward humanity, it's easy to look around at our world and become jaded toward God, cynical toward faith, and prematurely disappointed in the future. Many of us have chosen to identify with the pain of this life and have lost the will to believe in goodness again. We find it easier to believe in life's cruelty and deception.

I think this is why Jesus asked people if they wanted to be healed before He actually healed them. It can be more comfortable to stay in the brokenness we know than to step into the future we don't.

The Scriptures speak of a physically disabled man who had sat daily by a pool for thirty-eight years, waiting to be healed. When Jesus asked the man if he wanted to get well, this was his response:

> *"Sir," the invalid replied, "I have no one to help me into the pool when the water is stirred. While I am trying to get in, someone else goes down ahead of me."*
>
> ***—John 5:7***

Notice that he doesn't even answer the question. You would think that his response would be a quick and resounding "yes!" And, while His excuse may have been a valid one, the fact that he doesn't seem to be motivated to ask anyone to help him suggests that he might not be interested in being healed. Wholeness comes with risks and responsibilities that brokenness avoids.

It's easy to look at this man with judgement and see the

folly in his thinking, but how often do we do the same thing? How many times have we given into the thought that "this is just the way things are" or settled for a manageable life? Jesus is still asking the question to us today: "Do you want to get well?" Our response is often the same excuse as the man at the pool: "No one is helping me! Everyone else is getting ahead in life and I am just stuck here. These are just the cards that life has dealt me. It's not my fault!"

This perspective is problematic in two ways. First, it destroys any chance we have at moving forward in our faith journey. Anything good starts to look like a setup for more disappointment. Second, because we recognize the world's corruption, dishonesty, and cruelty, it becomes the context from which we live and make decisions.

We focus on the evil, or even the possibility of evil, and become blind to God's goodness. We perpetuate the problem by becoming corrupt, dishonest, and cruel –or worse, apathetic. Whatever shapes our perception determines who we become.

Working for Good

God never promised us that all things would be good. He never promised that life would be fair or easy. In fact, He informs us that trouble will be a consistent experience in this world. But He did promise us this: *"And we know that in all things God works for the good of those who love him, who have been called according to his purpose"* (Romans 8:28).

I love the motto of Patel, the hotel manager in the film

The Best Exotic Marigold Hotel: "Everything will be all right in the end. If it's not all right, it is not yet the end."[3]

Not everything will be good in your life, but God is in the process of working all things together for good. He's in the process of returning us to the goodness of Eden, where goodness is the norm, not the exception.

I was having coffee in town with a friend when a man stopped by our table. He stared at me, and, after a moment, he said, "Your name is Nathan, right?"

I listed off all the possible places where we may have met, but he told me that as he was passing our table, he heard a voice inside telling him my name and that he urgently needed to talk to me.

He began telling me his story: he was from Mexico, where he had been a world-class fashion designer. He had tailored suits for presidents, made robes for the boxing legend Muhammad Ali, and had his work displayed in museums around the world—you name it, he had achieved it. However, everything had fallen apart when he came to Los Angeles to care for his sick aunt. It turned out that she had lied about being ill, and now he was in an emotional and financial mess.

After hearing his heartbreaking story, I told him that God had sent him from Mexico to meet me at Mi Cafecito Coffee, so that he could once again find hope.

His name was Lazaro. I shared with him that he was named after a man in the Scriptures that had died and was brought back to life by his good friend, Jesus. It was clear that Jesus wanted to bring Lazaro back to life, too. By the end of our conversation, Lazaro had a life-altering encounter with God, fully stepping into a life of faith.

Lazaro spent several weeks with us in our home having dinners, joining in our community group and sharing conversations over more coffee. Slowly, things started shifting for him, but it started with how Lazaro was seeing his circumstances. What had once been roadblocks in his life became fuel for forgiveness, vision, and movement through the lens of God.

Lazaro moved away and we lost touch, but just the other day I saw him on Buenos Dias Familia online, talking about his fashion and faith. How beautiful is the goodness of God, to have brought Lazaro and me together in such a unique way, so that he and I could have experienced God work everything in Lazaro's life—even his business troubles and his aunt's deceit—for good.

Enhancing Our Faith with Goodness

If we are going to fully engage in this journey of faith, it's critical to enhance our faith with goodness, or the chaos of this world will consistently override faith in a loving God. We must resist the urge to give in to the darkness of cynicism and disappointment. We must retrain ourselves to believe that goodness is out there, and that God will work things out so that we can become the people He created us to be.

This is why the cross is so important. It's one thing for God to claim to be good. It's another thing for Him demonstrate that goodness. The pinnacle of His love and goodness was sending His Son to suffer and die for our brokenness, and to break the hold of death on humanity. Death is never the end of the story.

When we walk through our most painful moments, we can know that God is walking beside us. He understands what we are going through. His own Son suffered terribly, and He promises to transform our suffering into a powerful force of healing to bless others.

God created us good, and then made the way to sustain that goodness! The Scriptures say we are saved through faith, but that salvation is intimately linked with a command to bring goodness into the world. We are created to inhale God's goodness into our own souls, and exhale goodness to the world around us. True faith leads to goodness flowing out of us.

If we have confidence that God loves us always, we become powerful beyond measure. Supplementing our faith with goodness assures us of our future with God. No matter how dark the situation may seem, or what choices we have made, there is always hope because there is always goodness.

Chapter One Notes

CHAPTER TWO

Knowledge: The Power to Choose

The deed was done, and I was left burned. Literally.

No matter how many times my mom had warned me against it, my curiosity had lured me to learn for myself why this mysterious device was off limits. I can still vividly remember that moment when my understanding of "hot" went from a theory to a painful reality. There was no way I would ever touch that curling iron again and suffer the consequences!

If goodness is the enhancement that forms our perspective on faith, then knowledge reveals what we can trust as good. If we don't know what we're putting our faith in, there will always be a hesitancy to dive in with everything we have. Knowledge is what keeps us from getting burned over and over and keeps us grounded in what is true.

Moving in Faith

God is always speaking His truth to us, so that we can live the Godlike life we were made for—and that He desires for us. But until our faith is augmented by His knowledge, we'll never make progress toward participating with our divine nature.

Though faith is the way, 2 Peter 1:5–7 tells us that that faith must be enhanced with other spiritual qualities:

> *For this very reason, make every effort to add to your faith goodness; and to goodness, knowledge; and to knowledge, self-control; and to self-control, perseverance; and to perseverance, godliness; and to godliness, mutual affection; and to mutual affection, love.*

When we were expecting our first son, Jackson, I researched parenting and went into fatherhood with all kinds of theories. Sleep theories, feeding theories, attachment theories, even theories about diaper changing. But those theories went out the door when confronted with the reality of a screaming newborn and few hours of sleep. Life tests our ideas, and we find out what works—and what doesn't.

I'm fascinated by all kinds of theories and how people either adhere to or oppose them. For example, I used to raise chickens in our urban garden, and one day this question struck me: who first had come up with the theory that an egg might be edible? When they cracked open the shell and saw it was full of yellow slime, what on earth led them to put it in their mouth? They were either courageous, insane, or both.

That is why Scripture instructs us to add knowledge to our newfound perspective of goodness. Knowledge helps anchor our faith when our feelings are telling us to panic—when our emotions overwhelm us and we're teetering on the brink of despair. Knowledge helps our faith to be founded on facts, and not irrational reactions.

There is much grey area in our world that we would like to make black and white. However, God designed the world with many predictable realities and truths to live by. We know what time the sun will rise each day, to the minute. Tides come and go like clockwork. Seasons start and end in predictable ways. Gravity hasn't once failed us yet.

If God set up these physical, unaltering truths, then there must be some spiritual truths that are unchanging as well. It's our job to discover them so we can add them to our lives of faith.

My childhood friend Michael was an avid gamer. Of course, back then, Super Mario Brothers was about as good as it got. One day, we were defeating the evil empire of Bowser when Mike introduced me to a cheat code. Cheat codes were secrets that were built into the game that allowed the player to jump ahead in the game or gain an unfair advantage. With his cheat codes, we found ourselves transported from level three to level seven with the push of a few buttons.

The truths of God are like cheat codes (but not

cheating). They are secrets built into the game of life, and when we play by the right codes, we find ourselves moving further faster. This knowledge may not always allow you to bypass levels, but it certainly gives you an advantage in winning the prize.

In the Scriptures, Jeremiah tells us that our own thoughts and emotions are unreliable; they will lie to us: *"The heart is deceitful above all things and beyond cure. Who can understand it?"* (Jeremiah 17:9).

If our hearts are not currently believing that God is good, it becomes difficult for us to live out the truth that God is good. What we determine to be true is the reality in which we live.

Say, for example, that I've invited a group of people over to my home for a dinner party, and I tell them I will reveal a big surprise that night. Before the end of the evening, I've told half the group that I have a million dollars in cash that I'll be sharing between everyone in the room. The guests who have been told this are filled with happiness and excitement.

However, I've told the rest of the group that I plan to release a bag of venomous snakes. These guests are filled with anxiety, fear, and more than a little panic—especially when they learn that the doors will be locked and they'll be trapped.

That evening, when I bring out a bouquet of exotic flowers as my surprise, my guests' reality changes. The people who were expecting a big cash payout are now angry and depressed, and the people who were trying to find an escape route from the snakes are grateful and relieved.

The circumstances didn't change—I always had a

bouquet of flowers in mind—but everyone else's feelings and realities changed, based on their new knowledge.

If we're going to change our feelings, we must pursue the truth. We need to add knowledge to our perspective that God is good. Only when we believe God is good all the time and we can trust Him regardless of our circumstances, we can move in faith.

When Our Knowledge and Behavior Don't Match

What happens when our actions are not aligned with what we do know to be true? Though we hold certain beliefs about ourselves, others, and God to be true, our behavior often suggests otherwise.

Peter was one of Jesus' closest friends and most devoted followers. On the night before Jesus was murdered, when He told His followers what was about to transpire, Peter passionately declared that he would never betray Jesus. Later that night, Peter went as far as cutting the ear off a Roman soldier who was attempting to arrest Jesus. Yet less than twenty-four hours later, following Jesus' arrest, we find Peter denying he even knew Jesus. How did Peter get to this place within such a short period of time?

Paul sums up this dilemma in Romans:

> *I do not understand what I do. For what I want to do I do not do, but what I hate I do. And if I do what I do not want to do, I agree that the law is good. As it is, it is no longer I myself who do it, but it is sin living in me. For I know that good itself does not dwell in me, that is, in my sinful nature. For I have the desire to do what is good, but I cannot carry*

> *it out. For I do not do the good I want to do, but the evil I do not want to do—this I keep on doing. Now if I do what I do not want to do, it is no longer I who do it, but it is sin living in me that does it.*
>
> ***—Romans 7:15–20***

Does this sound familiar? Peter's duality may seem puzzling to many of us, but how often do we find ourselves doing the same? We know something to be true, and then immediately take actions that contradict our knowledge. Have you ever said or done something foolish, and, in the middle of actually doing it, had the thought, *"Why on earth am I doing this?"* The problem isn't always that we don't know the truth. The breakdown comes when our knowledge is in conflict with our basic nature.

The word *knowledge* comes from the Greek word *gnōsis*, which is also the word used to imply intimacy.[4] We become intimate with the beliefs we decide are true. They are like old friends that we grow increasingly comfortable and familiar with over time.

Growing up, we develop a series of beliefs and strategies that inform us about how to survive in this world—which people to associate with, which people to avoid, how to stay safe, and how to make ourselves look good. We become intimate with these truths, and they become the impetus for our actions and where we put our faith.

For example, I grew up in a very religious home, where happiness was celebrated, and anger was frowned upon. I learned early on that to survive this life I must keep up a smile and shove down feelings of injustice, hurt, or betrayal. The appearance of joy was protected at all costs, and I became intimate with this knowledge.

In many ways, this knowledge allowed me to survive in my family, and then through many circumstances in life. However, it also left me isolated and anxious at times, keeping a guard up against anything or anyone that was a threat to my looking good.

This intimate knowledge of self-survival will eventually come colliding into the faith-filled adventure that God invites us to. Safety and faith will always be at war within us. We were not made to simply live safe lives. The reality is, our most intimate knowledge wins.

Peter had knowledge of who Jesus was, but he also intimately knew what would keep him comfortable, protected, and in control. He found himself right in the middle of conflicting beliefs, and in that moment, the intimate knowledge of what would help him survive was more important to him than the knowledge of who Jesus was to him. Survival won.

And this conflicting knowledge shows up in so many places in life:

- I know that saving money for the future is wise, but I also know I want the latest model of the iPhone and to go on expensive date nights.
- I know that I should floss every day, but I also know that I want to sleep in those few extra minutes.
- I know that eating refined sugar isn't the best dietary choice I can make, but I also know that I love frozen yogurt.
- I know we're called to love others, but I also know

> how to put up walls in relationships to protect myself instead.

When two pieces of knowledge conflict, only one will prevail. You can't be financially secure and impoverished at the same time. Either you can have a good report at the dentist with no gum disease, or neglect flossing and sleep in.

Likewise, you can't move toward your divine nature and toward corruption at the same time. What you choose to supplement your faith determines which direction you move. As long as you remain stuck in this conflict, your future will look like your past.

Jesus promised us an abundant life. He is the One who gives more than we could ever ask or imagine. Our knowledge of God's goodness has the power to supersede any other knowledge we've gained.

So how do we supplement our perspective of God's goodness with knowledge in a way that resolves all this internal conflict? Second Corinthians 10:3–5 reminds us that we are in the midst of a spiritual battle and we fight spiritual battles with very specific weapons:

> *We demolish arguments and every pretension that sets itself up against the knowledge of God, and we take captive every thought to make it obedient to Christ.*
>
> ***—2 Corinthians 10:5***

Do you ever feel like you have a little lawyer in your head who is always arguing the case *against* a life of faith?

A lawyer's job is to win their case, and, in this case, he often is convincing us to play it safe and to look out for ourselves. The arguments can be convincing, but we must take that little lawyer captive, gagged and bound.

We grow out of a lot of things as adults, but one thing we never leave behind is our ability to imagine things. We often make up stories about ourselves, other people, and the world around us that are discouraging and untrue:

"I will never be able to succeed because..."

"People just can't be trusted because..."

"I'll never be as good as them, so I can't...

"God is constantly out to get me because..."

You may have told yourself one or more of those tales, and they serve a powerful and deceptive purpose. These stories give you permission to not have to do the hard work of examining where you are out of integrity with the knowledge of God. They often cause you to resign in desperation to "that's just the way things are."

"That's just how mom is."

"That's just how society is."

"That's just how the church is."

"That's just how I am."

These pretenses define both the present and the future, so faith becomes unnecessary. I don't need to take a risk if success is not a possibility for me. I never need to put myself out there if people can't be trusted. I never need to try if God is out to get me in the end. How many of us have settled for the comfort and predictability of our stories, forfeiting our birthright of greatness?

See how powerful the story is?

The good news is that you made them up, so you can take them down. We must take all these thoughts captive and align them with the voice of God, because they are actively trying to set themselves up against the knowledge of God. It may sound drastic, but getting rid of these thoughts is necessary. Our human default thinking is quite dissonant with the things of God.

Here's the good news: you don't have to believe everything you think! When you add knowledge about who God is to goodness, you are no longer enslaved to your errant thoughts. You can choose the knowledge of God at any given moment of life. Then you are free to move in the ways God is calling you and not spend precious energy worrying about the details.

How many people believe they aren't good enough and live their lives based on that knowledge? How many people believe they must perform to receive love? How many believe that if they give themselves away, they will be abandoned? How many think that God can't be trusted? If we give into those lies, and we live our lives based on them, we will be "destroyed from lack of knowledge" (Hosea 4:6).

Do you see how important knowledge is? We aren't destroyed due to a lack of power or resources, but knowledge. We are destroyed because we are not intimate with the mind of God, so we limit ourselves to our faulty human understanding.

Similarly, knowing the promises that have been made to us in Scripture changes everything. Here are a few examples:

- *"And we know that in all things God works for the good of those who love him, who have been called according to his purpose"* (Romans 8:28). Knowing that should give us confidence that even negative and painful experiences are being used to strengthen us.
- Knowing that God will fight for us and that no weapon forged against us will succeed (Isaiah 54:17) should change how we react to relational situations that we perceive as dangerous and unsafe. There's no need to run and hide anymore.
- Knowing that when we seek the Lord, He will deliver us from our fears (Psalm 34:4) should relieve some anxiety around our anxieties. You are being emancipated from all despair.
- There is no need to perform for His love. We are more than conquerors because He loves us (Romans 8:37). And nothing can separate us from His love (Romans 8:38–39).
- Knowing that the Spirit of Him who raised Jesus Christ from the dead lives in us (Romans 8:11) should change how we interact with every person and circumstance we encounter. You are made

powerful beyond measure in Christ.

That knowledge changes everything. When we are living those promises, we act according to God's plan. Knowledge changes our behavior and allows us to stand on something stronger than our feelings or circumstances. We stand in awe of Almighty God. Simply put, knowing the promises of Jesus enables us to participate in our divine nature.

You get to choose the knowledge you believe, and therefore the life you live.

Knowledge Leads to Action

Imagine you were given a map that showed you where to find a buried treasure worth millions of dollars. What would you immediately do?

Would you form a weekly study group in your home to analyze the map, section by section, for the next nine months, carefully deciphering each tiny nuance? Maybe you'd stop and spend your time and money on buying a building where you can gather a crowd to hear an expert share about the map in an eloquent and passionate manner each weekend. Still, maybe some of you would find a quiet place and meditate on the map and the treasure until it has really spoken to you.

Feel free to try any of these strategies while the rest of us get a shovel and start searching!

Scripture is our God-given map to engage the Godlike life we're longing for—the treasure in the field—and yet so few people seem to act on its promises. They study it, meditate on it, build buildings to speak about it, and thank God for it, but they never get around to taking hold of its promises and moving in faith. God tells us to go!

In Scripture, knowledge and faith are intimately connected. Much like intimacy, knowledge leads to action. Knowledge that is not lived out, is not put into practice, is useless. Paul tells us:

> *We continually ask God to fill you with the knowledge of his will through all the wisdom and understanding that the Spirit gives, so that you may live a life worthy of the Lord and please him in every way: bearing fruit in every good work, growing in the knowledge of God...*
>
> ***—Colossians 1:9–10***

We are filled with knowledge so that we can then live it. Knowledge without action is pointless and powerless. When we know the truth and fail to act, it often reveals an attitude of entitlement and arrogance that God wants to remove from our lives. Like spoiled children, we never fully recognize the powerful gift that we've been given, but simply wait for the next blessing that might come our way.

However, when we step out and start practicing the promises of God, it creates an atmosphere for His power and presence to flow through us.

Reverent Intimacy

> *The fear of the LORD is the beginning of knowledge, but*

fools despise wisdom and instruction.

—Proverbs 1:7

It's easy to forget how powerful and mighty and majestic God is. As the adage goes, familiarity breeds contempt. If we have any hope of living out the knowledge of God, we must maintain our fear of God. This is not fear in the sense of being terrified but fear in the sense of awe, reverence, and respect.[5]

My grandfather was the president of a bank and a wise, deeply respected, and dignified man. When I was a child, he sat me on his lap with our Diet Coke floats and talked to me about life—what choices I was making in school, future career goals, and what my plan was for the few dollars I had then. We shared a profound, loving intimacy, but I feared that man in the best of ways. Because of that, I took his word as true.

Similarly, our knowledge of God calls us into a loving intimacy characterized by reverence, awe, and respect. His truth becomes the plumb line by which we judge everything else. We know His truth by knowing His voice and the promises of Scripture that have proven themselves to be trustworthy through the ages.

We were designed to fully live, and the only way to fully live is to intimately *know* that God is good and to lean on that type of faith.

Enhancing Our Goodness with Knowledge

Goodness without knowledge makes us spiritually nearsighted. Spiritual and physical nearsightedness share some common challenges.

Before I had Lasik surgery, I was horribly nearsighted for thirty-five years, so I know firsthand the problems that come with this condition. First, I couldn't clearly see my hand three inches from my face, let alone accidents on the road or traffic jams, until I was right on top of them. Driving without my contacts or glasses wasn't even an option, as I would have inevitably crashed my car.

Second, I couldn't see something coming at me until it was too late to react. If someone threw a baseball at me, I wouldn't have known until it hit me in the face! I ended up nursing my wounds instead of being able to protect myself.

Spiritual nearsightedness comes with similar problems. When we're spiritually nearsighted, we can't see any further than our current circumstances because we are so focused on the moment. We lose our sense of the future and, with it, our ability to make choices affecting it in ways that enable us to find our divine nature. On top of that, spiritual nearsightedness blinds us from seeing how our choices will inevitably lead us into crashing our lives.

We also lose our ability to responsibly protect ourselves from attacks on our knowledge of God and render it ineffective. Remember, we live in a state of spiritual warfare, where our own thoughts set themselves up against the knowledge of God. We must take our own thoughts captive or else suffer blows from the enemy that we could have avoided.

If you are continually surprised by the negative results you are getting from your choices, chances are that you have grown spiritually nearsighted.

I once coached a young woman who wondered why all her dating relationships imploded when marriage became the next logical step. Each relationship lasted a few months, at most, despite the amazing chemistry she was experiencing. When I asked her if she became physically intimate with these guys early in the relationship, she said yes. Then I realized she had become spiritually nearsighted in her dating.

She agreed to an experiment I proposed. As soon as a guy made it apparent he was interested in having sex with her on a date, she would make it clear that she was going to wait for the spiritual commitment of marriage in a relationship before her physical commitment of sex.

After a year and a half, she came to see me again. This time she was married! This little experiment of ours helped her to distinguish between boys who were only interested in using her and men who were interested in being with her. Her new knowledge opened her eyes to see clearly who and what was in front of her, and it empowered her to make decisions that would lead to the future she longed for. She added knowledge to her act of faith.

If we feel God is disappointing us and we are discouraged by the outcomes in our lives, we may have just grown blind. The longer we stay in a place of spiritual nearsightedness, the more callous and disengaged we become until we lose our spiritual sight completely. Shame and guilt become our inheritance when we forget the truth that because we are connected to Christ our sins have been forgiven and are no longer counted against us.

What knowledge have you been ignoring or lacking that has been moving you toward corruption? It's time to enhance your newly refined perspective with the knowledge of God and His voice to determine what you put your faith in.

When you live in the knowledge that God is trustworthy and desires your good, it transforms your life. By enhancing your faith with goodness and then fortifying that perspective with the knowledge of God's truth, you can know the unknowable and be set free to participate with your divine nature.

God invites us to seek His knowledge so our faith can be enhanced. He wants us to move in and act on knowledge because it becomes the gateway to experiencing His power and presence in our lives.

Chapter Two Notes

CHAPTER THREE

Self-Control: Harnessing Your Greatness

I know that fast food is terrible for me, and yet, every so often, I find myself sitting in the drive-thru, scanning the menu. Many fast food chains have tried to offer healthier choices, but let's be honest—who goes to McDonald's because they're craving a salad? I imagine it's a pretty short list of people.

I've noticed that I find myself at fast food restaurants when I'm most vulnerable. I'm exhausted, discouraged, and I've taken a few blows in the battle of life. I want something that will comfort me, something I don't have to fight through or work hard for. An In-N-Out double with grilled onions and Animal-style fries usually does the trick.

Every time I engage in this ritual, I must go through the process of ignoring the knowledge that what I am putting in my mouth is completely unhealthy, devoid of actual nutrients and full of artery-clogging fat and cholesterol. I justify giving in to the temptation by telling myself that those facts really don't apply to me.

It really doesn't matter what we know if we are unwilling to align our lives with that knowledge. Without self-control, our knowledge is futile in moving us toward our divine nature.

So far, we've enhanced our faith with goodness, and that goodness with knowledge. The next supplement is self-control.

If *Schoolhouse Rock!* told us knowledge is power,[6] and Spiderman's Uncle Ben taught us that with great power comes great responsibility, then we must fully own the powerful responsibility of knowledge. Once we know that something is true, we must now do something with it. We can't go back to the way things were before and claim ignorance, because knowledge has shifted our reality.

James 4:17 phrases it like this: *"If anyone, then, knows the good they ought to do and doesn't do it, it is sin for them."* Once we know what is good, we must choose between what we know and what we want. Many times, those things are in opposition.

Knowledge Requires Self-Control

If you have a driver's license and know the rules of the road, then you should know that you must stop at red lights and stop signs. This may be a shock to some of you, but that law remains true even if you're in a hurry or frustrated behind the wheel, or if it's late at night and there are no other cars on the road. If you were to tell a traffic officer that you didn't feel like stopping at a stop sign, you can bet you are still getting that ticket. To act according to what you know, despite your emotions and your circumstances, you need self-control.

What we know to be true should determine how we live. When you choose to go against what you know, you miss the mark.

> If you know you are called to love others, and you choose indifference, you have missed the mark.
>
> If you know you are called to forgive, and you choose bitterness, you've missed the mark.
>
> If you know you are called to give, and you choose greed, you've missed the mark.

If we are going to live out the knowledge we've been given, then we must harness our passions, energy, and impulses to serve that truth. It is not about what feels good in the moment or what we think we can get away with. We must control our desires and align them with the reality that God has revealed to us. This is the definition of self-control.

Goodness and knowledge alone are not enough. It doesn't matter that you know the right thing to do if you don't live it out. Your action or inaction will then invalidate your knowledge and make it ineffective in moving you toward greater faith.

A few years ago, a good friend of mine was struggling with a new addiction, and I recognized how it was beginning to wreak havoc on his career and relationships. I mustered up the courage to get together and start this uncomfortable conversation. We discussed theological truths and practical realities of addiction, and I gave him some feedback on how it was affecting me personally. After the whole conversation, he sat back and surprised me with his answer:

"I understand and agree with everything you're saying, Nathan. I know this probably will end my career and hurt some very close relationships. But I'm not giving it up."

His answer was shocking, and to be completely honest, his transparency was a bit refreshing. He knew all the right answers, and I knew he could argue them even better than I on a cognitive level. However, he clearly had no intention of putting his knowledge into practice. He didn't even try to pretend. He knew the truth but had yet to become intimate with it in such a way that it compelled him toward self-control.

Knowledge is meant to produce change. If it doesn't, this is often because the element of self-control is missing.

The Guardian of Self-Control

Like a city whose walls are broken through is a person who lacks self-control.

—Proverbs 25:28

In the Old Testament, walls were built around cities to protect them. These walls served as the city's primary defenses in times of war and prevented enemies from invading.

If there was a breach in the wall, suddenly everyone and everything was vulnerable. Enemies could easily enter the city and steal the valuables, as well as kill or enslave the people.

In the same way, when we lack self-control, we become vulnerable to anxiety, despair, addiction, and other forms of spiritual darkness entering our lives. We're left paralyzed and unable to live the lives we long for and that God dreams for us.

When we choose not to control ourselves, all the blessings and gifts God has given us leak out of our lives. Self-control creates both a defensive and offensive barrier around our souls and gives us—and others—the opportunity to thrive.

It's Hard Work—but Worth It

Let's be real: out of all the enhancements Peter instructed us to add to our lives, self-control is the least appealing. Goodness, knowledge, godliness, love—even perseverance sounds like a much better party! Self-control just seems like hard work—and it can be.

But God never asks us to do something without abundantly providing the resources for it. Instead of looking at our own capabilities, we need to look to God to provide the level of self-control we need to produce the future we long for.

Notice how self-control is mentioned as a fruit of the Spirit in Galatians:

> *But the fruit of the Spirit is love, joy, peace, forbearance, kindness, goodness, faithfulness, gentleness and self-control. Against such things there is no law.*
>
> ***—Galatians 5:22–23***

We can identify a tree by the type of fruit it produces. When we bought our house, there was a beautiful orange tree in our backyard, but it didn't produce any fruit because the place where it had been planted was far too shady. Once we fertilized the soil and trimmed back the other trees to let the sun in, the tree's condition began to improve. Now that the orange tree was connected to sunshine, nutrients, and water, it began immediately producing oranges naturally and effortlessly, because that's what orange trees do in a healthy environment.

Look at the fruit of your life. If you are connected to the Spirit, your life will naturally produce love, patience, kindness, self-control, and so forth because you are connected to the source. Fruitfulness isn't something that we must strive for, but it should flow naturally as our spirit connects to a healthy environment.

As we spend time connecting with the voice of God, He will pour out everything we need from His Spirit into our spirits. Our essence starts to transform, becoming more like His. Although the rewards are great when this happens, the process can be painful, as He shows us the hidden areas in our lives that must change.

It is not enough to just know the voice of God. We need to allow His voice to control and guide our lives. God is not interested in just imparting information; He wants to transform the way we live. If we are willing to surrender to Him, He will continue to grow our faith and soon we find that self-control becomes second nature.

No Longer Victims

God calls us to control ourselves, but He doesn't leave us to do it in our own strength. Self-control occurs naturally in our lives when we are connected to Jesus, the source. Without self-control, we are victims to our emotions and our circumstances, helpless against a constant onslaught of temptation and discouragement that comes our way. The presence of self-control is evidence of our faith.

It's important to note, however, that God only asks us to control ourselves, not other people or situations. When we're unwilling to control ourselves, we end up shifting our energies into trying to control people or situations. Let's be honest. Deep down, most of us are control freaks.

Why is it that we'd rather control others than control ourselves? The reality is that we have absolutely no power to control another, and complete power to control our own lives, which often frightens us the most. God has given us the responsibility to govern ourselves, and we resist the weight of that responsibility. Attempting to control others becomes the perfect front for avoiding that power that comes with self-governance. Of course, when we resist the weight of that responsibility, we also forfeit the freedom that comes with it.

I have the privilege of coaching marriages when they are in breakdown, and the most common conversations I have are around submission and control. Often, both spouses are waiting for the other spouse to control themselves before they make any attempt at self-control, or they are trying to control their spouse and refusing to control themselves. Each spouse will often have a laundry list of things that need to change in their partner and are unwilling to hear the laundry list their spouse has for them.

This causes the marriage to come to an instant stalemate, which is no surprise. Imagine the frustration and futility of waiting for someone else to do what we're unwilling to do ourselves!

It only takes one person to create a new dynamic, and any of us can be that person, if we are willing to focus on controlling ourselves.

But what if we control ourselves and other people choose not to exercise self-control? That makes us vulnerable to others—to their impulses, their words, and their behavior. However, that same vulnerability opens a world of possibility for powerful relationships. All the energy that was once used to control and manipulate the other or keep things safe can now be used for love. Instead of focusing on the possibility of being hurt and giving in to the temptation to try to control others, we are freed to trust that God is big enough to heal and restore the relationship, time and time again.

When we exercise self-control, we are no longer

trapped as a victim to the action or inaction of others. Rather, we have freedom to move forward in all circumstances. As we control ourselves and experience God's abundant provision, our perspective changes.

The Freedom to Control Ourselves

We often think of exercising self-control as gritting our teeth and toughing it out. We associate it with self-denial and deprivation, with God limiting us in some way to white knuckle it through life.

Our God, however, is a God of freedom and abundance. John 8:36 tells us, *"So if the Son sets you free, you will be free indeed."* Shouldn't we be able to exercise that freedom?

We have this misconception that *freedom* means doing whatever we want. But if we are truly committed to freedom, it requires us being committed to the things that bring and sustain freedom. We must also be equally committed to resisting the things that would ensnare or enslave us. As Paul wrote, *"'I have the right to do anything,' you say—but not everything is beneficial. 'I have the right to do anything'—but not everything is constructive"* (1 Corinthians 10:23).

We can do whatever we want, but not everything will bring us freedom. Self-control is a critical component in living a life of complete freedom. With it, we have the freedom to decline those attitudes and actions that will ensnare us, and the freedom to engage what will keep us free.

Instead of looking at self-control as simply denying

ourselves things that we want, what if self-control was the engine that got you there faster? What if we saw self-control as an act of vision, a forward motion that brings us closer to the future we desire, and that God desires for us?

Marriage and family life can be difficult at times. There are plenty of opportunities for anger, frustration, arrogance, competitiveness, envy, and other destructive patterns to rear their ugly heads. Those attitudes will automatically create a very specific future for my family and me, a future I am not interested in creating. I know that if I am committed to have a thriving relationship with my wife and my sons, I must control my responses to those choices that will move me toward a corrupted future and away from my vision. Likewise, I must steward my responses toward life-giving attitudes and responses that foster the vision I have for my family.

God is always calling us into a bigger vision for what's next in our lives. Self-control is part of that. It's a spiritual practice that helps bring the tomorrow we long for into reality.

Enhancing Our Knowledge with Self-Control

As Paul tells us in 2 Timothy 1:7, *"For the Spirit God gave us does not make us timid, but give us power, love and self-discipline"*—that is to say, self-control.

These three qualities are intimately connected. You can't have power and love without self-control.

Without self-control, your Godlike power becomes destructive. Think of self-control as power harnessed for good. It is the ability to direct your power instead of it being a loose cannon and untamable. I have friends who break in horses and it's quite an intense and painful process. If a young horse isn't taught how to control its power and use it properly, the horse could cause harm to itself and its riders. Once tamed, its power is majestic and focused.

Similarly, God needs to break our selfishness, our old habits, and patterns of the past so that we can use His power for good instead of destroying ourselves and others. Without self-control, we will not use this power to create beauty in the world, only chaos.

Love without self-control becomes self-seeking and self-serving. It turns inward and becomes a means of taking from others rather than a means of giving to them. People are reduced to tools that are used to fill our needs.

With self-control, love becomes a force for good, a means of bringing healing and restoration to the world around us. It draws us closer to God—for God is self-controlled love—and to each other.

Self-control, when all is said and done, looks a lot like faithfulness to the things we know to be true, which is why it is necessary to enhance our knowledge with it. Self-control is doing the right things repeatedly and seeing our lives transformed as we maintain our connection with Jesus. When we restrain our lives to be in alignment with what we know to be true, momentum comes naturally.

Chapter Three Notes

CHAPTER FOUR

Perseverance: Becoming Invincible

My sister, Ruth, has been majestically tumbling, twirling, and flipping through the air since she was a young child. She knew early on that she would dedicate a significant amount of her life to competitive women's gymnastics (and significant would be an understatement). The teams and clubs she was a part of produced celebrated Olympic athletes.

Five days a week, Ruth went from school to the gym for workouts, practice, dance classes, and endlessly going over her competition routines. She returned home for dinner, homework, and then more stretching and icing sore muscles. The uneven bars, balance beam, floor, and vault became her life. We had makeshift gymnastics equipment in almost every room in our home growing up.

It was also very common for Ruth to come home limping with a sprained ankle, massive blisters on her palms, or completely discouraged from being unable to stick her landings after several dozen attempts that day. It was blood, sweat, and tears on a regular basis, and yet she returned the next day for more. Even after her coaches sat her down and gave her the heartbreaking news that her summer growth spurt would more than likely keep her from ever achieving her dream of competing with the U.S. Women's Gymnastics Olympic Team, she continued to show up for more torture.

Though chances were slim that Ruth would make it to the big games as a professional athlete and the physical toll was great, my sister displayed one quality necessary for us to activate our faith: perseverance.

After we've enhanced our faith with goodness, enhanced goodness with knowledge, and knowledge with self-control, we require perseverance, which is a close cousin to self-control.

We can usually stick to a healthy eating plan for week or drag ourselves to the gym for a few days in a row. But once we get beyond the short term, self-control becomes much more difficult.

The world is filled with dead resolutions that were never engaged long enough to transform lives. Living with this low level of integrity, we inevitably become bored, tired, discouraged, or completely lose trust in ourselves and others. Self-control becomes difficult and frustrating, leaving us exhausted and depressed.

Anyone can control themselves for a moment, but that doesn't count for much. We need to be willing to control our power and our love, even when it gets difficult, to harness it for a lifetime.

Perseverance is staying the course when it feels impossible to step into the future you were made to create, because at some point, self-control inherently turns into suffering. It will break you at some level and require part of you to die.

Suffering Is Part of the Game

Human beings have a natural tendency to avoid suffering. Left to our own devices, we default to keeping ourselves safe and comfortable, even if it means that we and our community pay a steep price for it.

Christianity has become a religion focused on comfort. We expect God to work around our work schedules, extracurricular activities, spending habits, and family needs. He would obviously never ask us to do anything awkward, uncomfortable, or inconvenient. He dare not mess with our finances. How did a faith that is centered around a God who was willing to sacrifice everything become so focused on making life convenient and manageable?

Scripture makes it clear that suffering is part of living a life of passionate faith, responding with anticipation as the voice of God calls us to risk everything. God is not a masochist, but suffering is the pathway to a transformed life—removing apathy and releasing hope. It shouldn't be a surprise that the words passion and suffering have the same etymology. Instead of trying to avoid suffering, we should press into it as a resource to stay the course.

> *But now, this is what the Lord says—he who created you, Jacob, he who formed you, Israel:*
>
> *"Do not fear, for I have redeemed you; I have summoned you by name; you are mine. When you pass through the waters, I will be with you; and when you pass through the rivers, they will not sweep over you. When you walk through the fire, you will not be burned; the flames will not set you ablaze."*
>
> ***—Isaiah 43:1–2***

This passage has been used throughout the years to inspire a sense of comfort and security. I've seen countless Bible covers with beautifully painted landscapes and this verse on them. Though security is certainly one aspect of this passage, it also tells us that intense chaos is inevitable in life.

We tend to forget that we must walk through the waters, pass through the rivers, and walk through the fire before we can reach the destination we long for. Yes, they will not overtake you, but who wants to experience the floods and fires of life? Ironically, I've never seen a motivational poster with images of flooded rivers and wildfires connected to this verse.

So often, we assume the waters, rivers, and fires are signs that God doesn't care and has abandoned us. The reality is, He promised the chaos! The power comes with the realization that He has equally promised to be with us as we walk through them. Knowing that we have a good God who is always with us is a game changer. That certainty creates an attractive context to persevere, even when our circumstances threaten to take us out.

This is one of the key differences between a relationship with Jesus and religion. Most religions are focused on avoiding or reducing suffering in this life. Jesus calls us to surrender and allow His Spirit to open our eyes to a whole new world of creative possibilities that exist when we let suffering move and strengthen us. When we stop resisting, all that energy is freed up to see how God might be with us in the suffering, using it to shape us.

Anything worth having in this life requires suffering or pain, and God invites us into that suffering with Him so we can have lives worth living. A beautiful intimacy develops when we are willing to enter that reality with others and with God. Persevering through suffering and difficult moments shapes us and helps us grow. Yet we waste so much time and resources avoiding the very thing that will lead to our glorious transformation.

We will willingly walk in faith until we come up against the waters, the rivers, and the fire. If we give up and refuse to persevere through their intensity, we miss out on the opportunity to participate with our divine nature. We must choose whether we will embrace suffering or resist it. We must choose to endure the pain of transformation or choose the pain of complacency.

Choose Your Pain

When the time came for my wife, Marla, to give birth

to our son, she opted for an unmedicated, natural birth with our midwife. My role in the birthing process was to coach her to surrender her body to the pain, stay connected to the vision of meeting our baby boy, relax, and persevere through it. Our birth instructor, Hallie, constantly reminded me that if she resisted the pain, she would slow down the birthing process, which would only prolong the suffering.

Though it is a natural—and perfectly understandable—human inclination, resisting pain leads to more pain. We need to allow pain to do what it's designed to do. Many of us spend so much energy resisting the discomfort of self-control and perseverance that we never enter it and instead create a new world of hurt for ourselves.

Like self-control, perseverance is a forward movement. It calls us into what is next—through the storm to the promise that awaits us on the other side. The suffering of perseverance isn't about refraining from doing something. It is not God depriving us or withholding from us. The suffering of perseverance is the crucible for birthing the vision that God has given us for our lives and the lives of others. It shapes us into the women and men needed to contain the future available on the other side.

> *Therefore, since we are surrounded by such a great cloud of witnesses, let us throw off everything that hinders and the sin that so easily entangles. And let us run with perseverance the race marked out for us, fixing our eyes on Jesus, the pioneer and perfecter of faith. For the joy set before him he endured the cross, scorning its shame, and sat down at the right hand of the throne of God. Consider him who endured such opposition from sinners, so that you*

will not grow weary and lose heart.

—Hebrews 12:1–3

God has marked out a race for each of us. It is not the rat race. It's not the nine to five mundane routine that many of us have settled for. It is far more than we could ever ask or imagine, going beyond the stresses and routines of daily life. It is a race for glory and hope, with a prize that is eternal, and perseverance is the key to running it to win.

Jesus had a clear vision for the redemption of humanity. He knew the race that was marked out for Him, and He ran it with perseverance. It was not easy—Jesus knew everything that had to happen to Him in order to achieve our salvation, and the agony of what was to come caused His sweat to be like drops of blood as He prayed for God to remove the ordeal He was about to endure. Even in that, He made a powerful request that God's plan would prevail over His desire to quit.

Jesus chose to persevere because love called Him into the future: *"For God so loved the world that he gave his one and only Son, that whoever believes in him shall not perish but have eternal life"* (John 3:16).

Jesus could have given up, but He pressed on because He had a vision of humanity being restored to a life-giving relationship with God.

Jesus will never ask us to persevere through anything that He Himself hasn't endured, and He will never ask us to do anything that He will not provide for. There is never a moment where He's wondering how He's going to get us out of or through a situation.

Jesus endured the cross, persevered unto death, and came back to life. He allowed the people He was serving to murder Him because of His love and His vision for a restored humanity.

Looking at this through a modern psychological lens, it's easy to think that God has some severe boundary issues. However, we are the ones with unhealthy boundaries. We tend to be overly concerned with protecting ourselves—making sure our needs are met, making sure our comfort is prioritized, making sure our preferences are respected. We often set boundaries to make sure we remain safe at all costs, rather than setting boundaries for love to thrive.

Self-protection is one of the greatest enemies of perseverance. We cannot persevere when we are trying to protect our own priorities or agenda. Jesus calls us to persevere through suffering without trying to defend ourselves or our needs. That's His responsibility in the process—and why He walks with us in it.

Just as a woman giving birth is instructed not to resist the pain of bringing a baby forth, we are not to resist the pain of stepping into the future to which we are called. We get to choose between the pain of resisting the future and the pain of bringing forth a future of hope.

The Byproduct of Hope

I love the phrasing used in Hebrews 12:1, that if we are to run our race and persevere, we need to "throw off everything that hinders." As we do, we discover that perseverance produces hope.

- We throw off unforgiveness for relationship and find the hope of intimacy.
- We throw off bitterness for compassion and find the hope of freedom.
- We throw off anger for joy and find the hope of openness.
- We throw off apathy for action and find the hope of fullness.
- We throw off pride for humility and find the hope of authenticity.
- We throw off greed for generosity and find the hope of gratitude.
- We throw off envy and comparison for family and find hope in community.
- We throw off comfort for obedience and risk and find the hope of wholeness.
- We throw off just getting by for life and find the hope of loving fully.

We must do whatever it takes to throw off what hinders us and walk through the storm. Scripture emphasizes the connection between hope and persevering through suffering:

> *Not only so, but we also glory in our sufferings, because we know that suffering produces perseverance; perseverance, character; and character, hope. And hope does not put us to shame, because God's love has been poured into our*

hearts through the Holy Spirit, who has been given to us.
—Romans 5:3–5

If we find ourselves in a hopeless place, chances are that God is calling us to persevere. Hope is produced during our willingness to persevere. When we persevere and throw off the baggage hindering us, we begin to see and experience the beautiful plan God has designed for our lives.

Enhancing Our Self-Control with Perseverance

We don't always know why we face troubles in this life, but we can always trust God has a purpose for our circumstances. Often, we can look back and see His blessings because together we trudged through the darkness to reach the sunrise. However, it is hard to see the sunrise when we are focused on the lack of light in the moment.

Life in ministry is not for the faint of heart. As the leader of a faith community, I find that there's often a lot of criticism—some of it deserved, some of it undeserved—and I frequently feel pulled in different directions all at once. There are days where it feels like a fight to get out of bed and face the impossibility of meeting the expectations that others have on me.

Years ago, I asked a friend and mentor of mine, Jean-Marie Jobs, to coach me through a season in my leadership where I felt apathetic, fearful, and stuck. She challenged me to list everyone that had hurt me in some way and that I was struggling to forgive. By the end of the day, I had a list of 147 specific names in my journal. I remember looking at that list and thinking that a normal desk job sounded really appealing. Why on earth would I put myself and my family through that type of hurt?

But then, there are those moments where people share with my wife and me about how we played a part in leading them to find a meaningful connection with Jesus. Just the other day, a woman was weeping in our living room, sharing how she would be dead without our ministry and the community it has created.

We've seen countless individuals freed from addiction, anxiety, and depression and healed from all types of physical pain and disabilities. Marriages and families found their start in our Sunday gatherings, with new legacies being born. These eternal victories far outweigh any temporary hurts I've suffered and call me into greater levels of forgiveness and perseverance.

I have a vision for a community of faith that is known by its love and that stands with others to persevere through any suffering that gets in between them and their divine nature. This will always be a community where here we can truly press on because of the hope that we share, creating life amid any difficulties. The Apostle Paul encourages us to persevere and stay the course: *"Let us not become weary in doing good, for at the proper time we will reap a harvest if we do not give up"* (Galatians 6:9).

Perseverance never happens in a vacuum, but always in the context of community. It's ironic that our first reaction is to isolate ourselves in the storm when people are the resource that Jesus uses to help us through it. Yes, people are messy and complicated and don't often show up the exact way we want them to. Many times, it's people who create the need for perseverance! However, the glory of "us" always outweighs the pain and exhaustion of fighting the fires and floods alone.

Love must pull us through, so that at the end of our lives, we might claim, *"I have fought the good fight, I have finished the race, I have kept the faith"* (2 Timothy 4:7).

So many people reach the end of their lives and realize they gave up on the race for godliness years ago. Fighting through the storm teaches us things that we otherwise would never have known and changes our perspective on the other side. We are then freed to live and love because we have a God who has done the same.

By enhancing our self-control with perseverance, we develop a lasting faith that will pull us through. We were designed to not only withstand the storm in the presence and power of Jesus but to have the storm shape us and our faith into a powerful witness of God's love. We were made to be invincible against anything that gets between us and the future we were called to create.

We may never be an Olympic gymnast, but God calls and trains us to run a higher race for His good purpose. When we persevere through the race, then God shows us the beauty of our reward.

Chapter Four Notes

CHAPTER FIVE

Godliness: Rising Above

I learned early on in my life that I had a gift for language. Communication is among my top five talent themes on Gallup's CliftonStrengths assessment, and I don't often find myself struggling to put thoughts into words or influencing people with them. I did not, however, always use this talent in a constructive way. As a kid, I could cut people down to size in a moment with my sharp tongue. I couldn't throw a punch to save my life, but my insults hurt worse than any uppercut.

When relational storms came, I ended up lashing out at people verbally. Bitterness and contempt flowed like a burning poison from inside me, flooding my life and threatening to drown me and everyone else unlucky enough to be in my wake. The frightening thing was how fast and easy they overflowed from my heart, even as a young adult.

One day, after making a complete fool of myself with my words in front of the leadership of my father's church, I decided that, instead of wielding this gift like a sword to attack others, I would endure the pain and hurt of relationships in a more resourceful way. I found greater levels of compassion and understanding toward others, and I was able to elevate my relationships instead of destroying them. I had to choose to persevere when things got difficult, choosing godliness over dishonor.

We have already added the enhancements of goodness, knowledge, self-control, and perseverance. Each supplement builds on the next. We can't persevere until we've decided to control ourselves. We can't control ourselves until we have knowledge of what God is asking us to control within ourselves, and we can't trust that knowledge unless we know that God is good. All of this requires faith.

The next part of the journey is godliness. We must add godliness to our perseverance if we're ever to participate with our divine nature. Godliness is the act of becoming like God by taking on His characteristics and His attributes so that our lives reflect His. This is not something we can achieve on our own—Godlikeness can only come from God Himself.

We Are Not God

Our human default is to take on the role of God in our story. There is a longing to be the masters of our own universe, much like Adam and Eve. This is especially evident when we're children. We're born believing ourselves to be the center of our worlds—and we have an innate ability to manipulate our circumstances and other people to ensure that's the case.

I have always been amazed at Jackson's ability to control and negotiate to get what he wanted from a very early age. It's like he came into this world with a built-in device which could twist our hearts around his finger when he wanted something. Whether it was the cookie, the pacifier, or the extra few minutes with his apps on our phone, he could turn on the lower lip and waterworks at the drop of a hat. It was equally amazing to see how fast he could shut them off when his demands were met and hostages were released.

The funny thing is, we never really grow out of that mindset; we just develop more tools and tactics to achieve our goal of staying in control, meeting our own needs, and keeping ourselves comfortable.

As a result, we end up trying to compete with God, testing our wills against His. Ironically, there is no need to fight with Him, as He is actively inviting us to share in His godliness—not to become a god but to submit to Him as God and become Godlike through that surrender. In the process, He gives us His Spirit and His power, love, and self-control.

We're already created with divine spiritual DNA. He

simply wants to complete the picture by making us more like Him.

Becoming Godlike

So, how do we become more like God? First Corinthians 2:10–11 offers some insight:

> *...these are the things God has revealed to us by his Spirit.*
>
> *The Spirit searches all things, even the deep things of God. For who knows a person's thoughts except their own spirit within them? In the same way no one knows the thoughts of God except the Spirit of God.*

At first, this sounds like a losing proposition. If no one knows God's thoughts except for His Spirit, how on earth are we supposed to become Godlike without knowing His thoughts? We can make assumptions or attempt to mimic His behavior, but it's hard when we physically can't see the God we are trying to become more like.

We often try to fill in the gaps with our own thoughts on how to become Godlike. We think that if we know enough about God, we will become like Him. But God is not interested in our memorizing and sermonizing; knowledge alone is not enough. We can be convinced that if we just do enough good things, or if the good outweighs the bad, then we will be Godlike. However, Jesus doesn't spend a lot of time or energy on behavior modification in His teachings.

Romans 3:10 reminds us that *"there is no one*

righteous, not even one," while Romans 3:23 takes it a step further, asserting that *"all have sinned and fall short of the glory of God."* We have all missed the mark. We are incapable of producing what is needed to live Godlike lives on our own. Knowledge and good behavior will not save us from our corrupted state.

Thankfully, God provided a way for us to know His thoughts: *"What we have received is not the spirit of the world, but the Spirit who is from God, so that we may understand what God has freely given us"* (1 Corinthians 2:12).

When we engage a relationship with Jesus, His Spirit begins to work *in* us and helps us know and understand the essence of the divine. The moment we surrender to Him, our corruptible nature is redeemed, and His vibrant, all-knowing Spirit is transplanted into us, equipping us with everything we need to live Godlike lives—for both our day-to-day life as well as storms.

Paul took this conversation a step further: *"... 'Who has known the mind of the Lord so as to instruct Him?' But we have the mind of Christ"* (1 Corinthians 2:16). When we decide to add godliness to our perseverance, we gain access to the mind of Christ. With this new advantage, we can know the deep things of God.

On our own, we are hopeless and helpless to attain the Godlike state we were designed for, but Christ has gone before us, paying the ultimate price to give us the pathway to this life and godliness. It is impossible for us to live a Godlike life apart from Jesus.

Temptation or Trial?

When we find ourselves persevering through a storm, we tend to ask ourselves whether the storm is a temptation or a trial. It's safe for us to assume God wants to use every storm as a trial. As we pass through it, what's inside us is both refined and revealed. It only becomes a temptation when we fail to persevere and refuse to allow the storm to elevate us.

We can look back on our lives and see how we have allowed specific events to shape us. That is what perseverance is designed to do—in fact, it's one of the main tools God uses to refine us.

It's important to note that perseverance—going through the experience that required us to engage our faith in the first place—is not the endgame. Persevering for the sake of perseverance doesn't make much sense. We call that masochism. Perseverance in the context of a vision for our lives is a powerful spiritual force.

That the storm will shape us is inescapable. The bigger question is: how will we allow ourselves to be shaped? What is God seeking to do in and through our lives during these times?

God isn't interested in playing games; there is a purpose in every trial He allows in our lives. How we persevere determines the outcome. The goal isn't simply to get to the other side of the storm. Anyone can survive.

No one is really after the participation award in this life. We long for the prize! The goal is for perseverance to transform and elevate us, for us to look more and more like God by allowing Him to shape us so we might win.

We already looked at how perseverance and hope are connected in Romans 5, but that passage also shows how suffering produces godly character in us:

> *Therefore, since we have been justified through faith, we have peace with God through our Lord Jesus Christ, through whom we have gained access by faith into this grace in which we now stand. And we boast in the hope of the glory of God. Not only so, but we also glory in our sufferings, because* ***we know that suffering produces perseverance; perseverance, character****; and character, hope.*
>
> **—Romans 5:1–4**

In a word, the goal of persevering through suffering is Godlike character.

Have you ever seen two people go through the same difficult circumstances and come out dramatically different from each other on the other side? One person thrives despite a serious health issue, job loss, or tragedy and comes out stronger, wiser, and more loving. The other person, however, withers and comes out with addictions, bitter, resentful, and angry.

What we do in the storm determines our destination. Adding godliness to our perseverance keeps our struggle from being wasted. Far too many of us simply endure life rather than persevering, allowing God to shape us through the storm and make us into the people He intended us to be. How many of us waste our suffering? A storm may very well be the greatest gift He could ever give us to become Godlike.

God will never waste our wounds. Perhaps He's

waiting for us to do the same.

Enhancing Our Perseverance with Godliness

When we find ourselves in the storm, our good works and rituals mean very little. God is not interested in performance; He is interested in godliness. Consider what Jesus says to the Pharisees, religious leaders who were known for their outward adherence to God's law:

> *Woe to you, teachers of the law and Pharisees, you hypocrites! You are like whitewashed tombs, which look beautiful on the outside but on the inside are full of the bones of the dead and everything unclean. In the same way, on the outside you appear to people as righteous but on the inside you are full of hypocrisy and wickedness.*
>
> ***—Matthew 23:27–28***

Thankfully, God doesn't want to leave us in that position. If perseverance is the friction that both removes and reveals what's inside of us, it will bring out both the beautiful and the broken. Godliness comes through persevering with the mind of Christ. If we allow Him, He will transform our chaos into beauty.

> *You were taught, with regard to your former way of life, to put off your old self, which is being corrupted by its deceitful desires; to be made new in the attitude of your minds; and to put on the new self, created to be like God in true righteousness and holiness.*
>
> ***—Ephesians 4:22–24***

It's not enough to just persevere. Like an eagle, we need to fly into the storm and use it to elevate our position. By actively choosing to put off our old selves and putting on the things of God, we can leverage the hardships of this life and allow them to transform us into the godly, beautiful people God created us to be.

Chapter Five Notes

CHAPTER SIX

Mutual Affection: The Art of Empathy

There are a lot of ideas and sayings in our culture that we accept as true without really considering their accuracy. For example, we tend to think that loving someone means being nice to them. Jesus, however, wasn't focused on being nice at all; He spoke the truth in love and told people what they needed to hear. In that way, He was kind, but certainly not nice.

Speaking the truth in love often required Jesus to use intense language. Jesus called His closest friend, Peter, "Satan" at one point, and He referred to the religious leaders as a "brood of vipers" on multiple occasions. His words were not intended to insult but to stir up a spiritual response.

Another phrase we've bought into is "I love you, but I don't like you." How is that even possible? Loving someone is a much higher commitment than liking someone. It's like saying, "I would sacrifice everything for you, but I won't give you the ten dollars in my wallet." See the irony? This also reveals the mental games we play at times when it comes to truly loving our neighbor.

This is the part in the journey where the rubber meets the road. Thus far, we have added to our faith goodness, to goodness knowledge, to knowledge self-control, to self-control perseverance, and to perseverance godliness. All these enhancements have been about us—they've focused on who we are becoming as individuals. Our next enhancement, *mutual affection*, takes our godliness and orients it outward, directing it toward others and the relationship we have with them.

It All Relates

Almost everything in life comes back to relationships. Just as the relationship between the moon and the earth affects the tides and the relationship between the sun and the earth affects the seasons, our spiritual life is all hinged on relationship.

Therefore, we shouldn't be surprised that our faith eventually must move outward, affecting not only us but those around us. Anything that is worth having faith for is usually connected to a relationship. For example, any faith

I have for my health, my finances, and my life circumstances is intimately connected to the relationship with my wife, sons, and community. Everything that affects me has a direct and indirect effect on them as well.

God moves us toward relationship. He makes us whole, powerful, spiritually healthy, and Godlike so that we can then give all of that away and spend ourselves on behalf of others in our lives.

In our home, we have a large piece of art in the dining room that reads "Give your life away." It's one of the first things I see each morning, and it reminds me that my purpose is to sacrifice for those around me. It has become the culture we strive to create with our family and at Humanity Church.

However, due to our natural human inclination toward scarcity and shame, we tend to love poorly when left to our own disposition. Love begins at the very basic level of having affection for one another, which is why this enhancement can only be added after we've engaged godliness.

The Greek word *philadelphia* means "brotherly love, brotherly kindness, and love of the brethren."[7] It is a familial love, being with others as if they are your own flesh and blood. It is translated as "mutual affection" in some translations of the Bible. This specific Greek word is only used five times in Scripture.

Mutual is defined as "a feeling or action experienced or done by each of two or more parties toward the other or others."[8]

Affection is defined as "a feeling of liking and caring for someone or something: tender attachment."[9]

We can therefore define *mutual affection* as caring for and being attached to one another. How radical would it be if we *lived* and loved as if we were spiritually connected to one another as one? The reality is, we are.

Unity in the Church

The church is a fascinating social experiment. It calls together people from radically different ethnicities, genders, races, age groups, political affiliations and perspectives—people who normally wouldn't have any reason to be together. The church then connects us to Jesus and tells us that, through this relationship, we are to be knit together and come to love one another as we love ourselves.

It sounds like the premise for a reality show that is destined to be a hot mess, but this is the context to which God calls us. Paul explains what it should look like when followers of Jesus come together:

> *Be completely humble and gentle; be patient, bearing with one another in love. Make every effort to keep the unity of the Spirit through the bond of peace. There is one body and one Spirit, just as you were called to one hope when you were called; one Lord, one faith, one baptism; one God and Father of all, who is over all and through all and in all.*
>
> ***—Ephesians 4:2–6***

The spiritual reality is that the moment we connect to Jesus, we are moved from a group of individuals into a "one"—one body, one Spirit, one hope, one faith, one baptism, and one Father. This dynamic can only be achieved through the power of God and a dirty word in our culture: *submission.*

This oneness within the body of believers often violates our sense of personal rights, and we bristle against the humility required. Americans suffer from a strong case of chronic individuality. We've been indoctrinated from a young age to chase down our personal dreams at all costs and not let anyone or anything stop us from pursuing our own happiness. What is more American than that?

We must rail against this cultural conditioning if we have any hope of finding the unity and intimacy our souls are longing for. Notice the extreme language that Paul uses: *"Be* ***completely*** *humble"* and *"Make* ***every*** *effort."* This isn't just encouragement to give it a shot. This is a mandate to keep persevering until it happens—so it's a good thing we just engaged that enhancement!

How many of us gesture toward unity but then walk away discouraged or angry because we tried and it didn't turn out the way we wanted on the first or second attempt? Maybe we gave it a real go, but eventually stopped when it wasn't fun anymore. "I tried" is one of the greatest enemies to the mutual affection needed if we're ever going to reach the oneness that Scripture commands.

Remember that each of us carries a piece of the spiritual DNA of God. If we allow those pieces to be submitted to one another, we experience a much greater picture of the fullness of the divine.

Likewise, your personal dreams and longings are not in opposition to the greater vision that God has for you in a community. On the contrary, when we submit those dreams and longings as an offering to both God and one another, the result is often far greater than the original dream. God will never call you to give up something that He won't return or replace with something beyond what you could ask or imagine. He is in the business of elevating, not diminishing.

When we connect to Jesus, it transforms us and gives us everything we need to live together in peace and love. Then, and only then, can we come from and celebrate diverse backgrounds, yet be united with genuine mutual affection for one another. This is the communal foundation for the life you and I were made to live!

The Price of Unity

We are called to maintain the unity of the Spirit by living in peace with each other and bearing with one another in humility, gentleness, and patience. This is not our default setting; human nature is self-focused and impatient.

It makes sense that we tend to think of modern spirituality as a private matter. At best, we engage in self-preservation by trying to pick and choose who gets to make up the church based on our preferences. At worst, we may decide to go on our spiritual journeys completely alone, never integrating into a body where we invest in others and allow others to invest in us. It's not necessarily easier, but it feels more comfortable and much less complicated. We're never fully known, but never have to be inconvenienced in our faith.

However, being a part of the local church and striving for unity is powerfully transformative. It creates an atmosphere where everyone is in pursuit of living in mutual affection for each other and provides a beautiful context for hope, freedom, and faith. We may fool ourselves in believing that going it alone is the greatest path to liberation, but, the natural result is isolation and loneliness – a smaller life.

And yes, working toward unity is also a context for disappointment, betrayal, and hurt. We are guaranteed to suffer when we decide to knit ourselves together. It's a given that we will eventually be hurt by others, because it is a given that you and I will eventually hurt others.

Ironically, one reason for this is that we expect others to do and be for us what we know we cannot do and be for them. We expect others to be a perfect, unending source of care and connection, and we often feel offended and betrayed when they let us down: "They didn't return a text on time. … He didn't say hello to me this morning. … She rubs me the wrong way." And yet, we're shocked when someone tells us that we've let them down in the same fashion.

To successfully live out the reality of unity and pursue mutual affection, we must be filled with grace and forgiveness—qualities that seem to be in short supply today. We live in a world that is constantly offended by the small things. Our fuses are shorter than ever, and our claims to our rights are our biggest priority.

Unwilling to submit and lay down our offense, we lack the capacity to hold a space for grace and forgiveness toward others on our own. Despite how connected we are through technology and social media, we find ourselves alone, isolated, and anxious.

Practicing Mutual Affection

So how are we to engage this enhancement of mutual affection, especially since we have such a limited supply of it on our own? It's a good thing that we just added godliness to our perseverance, because we must be Godlike in order to live in a consistent place of grace and forgiveness for those around us. That is how He relates to us. By persevering and then adding godliness, we're able to extend to others the abundance of grace and forgiveness needed to create an environment where mutual affection can thrive.

Ephesians 4:25–32 gives us insight into what mutual affection looks like:

> *Therefore each of you must put off falsehood and speak truthfully to your neighbor, for we are all members of one body. 'In your anger do not sin': Do not let the sun go down while you are still angry, and do not give the devil a foothold. Anyone who has been stealing must steal no longer, but must work, doing something useful with their own hands, that they may have something to share with those in need.*
>
> *Do not let any unwholesome talk come out of your mouths, but only what is helpful for building others up according to their needs, that it may benefit those who listen. And do not grieve the Holy Spirit of God, with whom you were sealed for the day of redemption. Get rid of all bitterness, rage and anger, brawling and slander, along with every form of malice. Be kind and compassionate to one another, forgiving each other, just as in Christ God forgave you.*

The beautiful thing is that God never asks us to step

into something He hasn't stepped into Himself, and He provides everything we need for success. As we take on godliness, we are equipped with everything we need to be mutually affectionate toward each other.

Therefore, the progression of the enhancements we find in 2 Peter is so important. The process naturally builds on itself, so it's vital not to skip any steps along the journey.

It's like putting together a piece of furniture from IKEA—you have to follow the process; you can't just jump to the endgame. I've tried this technique many times, to save time. I have inevitably ended up with a door on backward or several leftover pieces—causing me to spend double the time it would have taken to follow the directions.

There are no shortcuts in this journey, but there is great reward for those who complete it.

Enhancing Our Godliness with Mutual Affection

It is impossible to have mutual affection unless we have first persevered with godliness. Experiencing a storm in our lives and seeing God pull us through humbles and fills us with grace, forgiveness, and compassion. We find ourselves with greater understanding for others, knowing that God is with them on their journey, just as He was with us on ours.

By persevering with godliness, we also discover that God will continue to redeem us as we enter the pain, suffering, and betrayal of relationships. Though pain is inevitable, we are empowered to enhance our godliness with mutual affection because we have a God who continues to heal us and is an endless source of grace and forgiveness.

In Romans 12:10, we find another use of the Greek word *philadelphia* in Scripture: *"Be devoted to each other with mutual affection. Excel at showing respect for each other"* (ISV). Another version translates the verse this way: *"Be devoted to one another in love. Honor one another above yourselves"* (NIV).

It makes sense that honor is connected to mutual affection. The word honor in Hebrew, *kabod*, means to make weighty. When we exchange mutual affection, we give weight and gravitas to the other person. They are no longer a thing to be easily used, dismissed, or disregarded, but a carrier of divine DNA.

In this way, we elevate humanity through mutual affection. Honor shifts relationships from mere interactions to a compelling partnership that achieves the purposes of God on earth. Honoring the other is a powerful demonstration that we no longer need to be in competition with or live in protection from one another. The honor that comes with mutual affection deepens the human experience and opens powerful possibilities for creating the future we long for, together. We were designed for oneness.

Mutual affection—filled with honor, forgiveness, and grace—looks a lot like empathy. When we start caring for one another as if we are one, we begin to see struggles, suffering, and sin as *our* struggles, suffering, and sin. There is no room to set things up as an us versus them in the game in life. We recognize that we are just as much in need of a Savior as our enemy.

Mutual affection creates a tribe of brothers and sisters around us. We are not meant to make the journey of faith alone; we are meant to be connected to each other and live together in a space of faith. With this type of united front, we become an indestructible force of good.

It is only in mutual affection that we can participate in *our* divine nature, giving and receiving grace, compassion, and empathy to and from our brothers and sisters in the same way we receive them from God. If we all lived like that, surely humanity would look more like God envisioned it when He said, "It is very good."

Chapter Six Notes

CHAPTER SEVEN

Love: Becoming Godlike

"I don't think you actually love me."

When my wife, Marla, and I first began dating, everything seemed to be going smoothly, but then those seven words cut like a knife. I was ticked off.

Despite everything I had invested in our relationship—spending most of my time with her, having hours of meaningful conversations, paying for budget-breaking dates—she wasn't sure I really loved her? What more could she possibly want from me?

I'm not a touchy-feely guy. In fact, I don't think physical touch shows up anywhere on my list of love languages,[10] so it didn't naturally occur to me to hold her hand when we were walking down the street or to sit close to her on the couch when we were watching a movie. My preference is for lots of personal space and fresh air. But for Marla, those actions would truly express love to her. After several years of marriage, I am convinced she experiences love almost exclusively through physical touch.

So I wrote reminders in my phone with an alarm to hold her hand or put my arm around her "impromptu" when we were watching Netflix. Even though these weren't things I would've instinctively done on my own, I chose to engage in them passionately because I was committed to Marla knowing and experiencing how much I loved her.

Until I sacrificed my preferences to meet her needs, my words and actions didn't mean anything to her. Once I did, everything shifted—she realized I did fully love her, and we were engaged a few months later.

We have enhanced our faith with goodness, knowledge, self-control, perseverance, godliness, and mutual affection. Everything on this journey has been preparing us for this final glorious destination. Love is the final enhancement.

Love is a fitting end to this list of enhancements, and it stems from mutual affection. We cannot fully love others until we have engaged empathy, care, and connection with one another. From that foundation, we can then dive into the deeper love that becomes available to us through Christ.

What Is Love?

The word *love* is used in so many ways—I love coffee, I love my wife, I love a great idea. How can we define a word that carries so many shades of meaning?

> *Dear friends, let us love one another, for love comes from God. Everyone who loves has been born of God and knows God. Whoever does not love does not know God, because God is love. This is how God showed his love among us: He sent his one and only Son into the world that we might live through him. This is love: not that we loved God, but that he loved us and sent his Son as an atoning sacrifice for our sins. Dear friends, since God so loved us, we also ought to love one another. No one has ever seen God; but if we love one another, God lives in us and his love is made complete in us.*
>
> *This is how we know that we live in him and he in us: He has given us of his Spirit. And we have seen and testify that the Father has sent his Son to be the Savior of the world. If anyone acknowledges that Jesus is the Son of God, God lives in them and they in God. And so we know and rely on the love God has for us.*
>
> *God is love. Whoever lives in love lives in God, and God in them. This is how love is made complete among us so that we will have confidence on the day of judgment: In this world we are like Jesus. There is no fear in love. But perfect love drives out fear, because fear has to do with punishment. The one who fears is not made perfect in love.*
>
> *We love because he first loved us. Whoever claims to love God yet hates a brother or sister is a liar. For whoever does not love their brother and sister, whom they have seen, cannot love God, whom they have not seen. And he has given us this command: Anyone who loves God must also love their brother and sister.*
>
> ***—1 John 4:7–21***

Philadelphia love moves us toward mutual affection, but the love John wrote about in this letter is on a much deeper spiritual level. *Agape* is the Greek word used above and it describes the love of the divine. This love is an unending sacrificial force that chooses to give itself freely to the object of its affection. This is the love that believes all things, hopes all things, and endures all things. This is the love that never fails (1 Corinthians 13).

We can categorically say that God is agape love because He has sacrificed for us. His love is not based on a feeling or a question. We can point to the moment in history when God took on flesh and both physically and spiritually sacrificed Himself so that we could live. This is love: God gave.

When someone is giving themselves to you, it is an unforgettable experience. One evening several years ago, I was sitting in a mentor's home watching an anticipated new episode of *Lost*. They had just installed this brand-new technology called a TiVo where we could fast forward through commercials. My mind was absolutely blown! What would they come up with next?

At the end of the evening, I simply said, "I have to save up and get a TiVo!" My friends immediately walked over to the television, unplugged the unit and handed it to me with a full-year paid subscription. "We'll get another one," they said, and sent me on my way home. I was speechless.

Sitting in the car that night, I knew I was loved. I knew this, not because they had given me a new toy, but because they had chosen to sacrifice for me. It wasn't just a feeling or a question. I was loved. When someone sacrifices to give you something, you don't question their love. This love is the most powerful force on the planet.

God is the essence of sacrificial agape love, so we were made from and for agape love. When God breathed life into us, He breathed in His goodness and sacrificial love. Knowing this makes all the difference in the world for how we live. When we are blind to this, we end up wasting our energy and time trying to figure out our purpose in life.

I remember building a chicken coop in our yard and misplacing my hammer in the process. Instead of taking the time to find it or go buy a new one at the hardware store, I decided to use a big rock I found nearby to bang in about a hundred nails. It was a clunky, awkward, and exhausting process with a tool that was never designed to be used for that purpose. The project took about three times as long and ten times the energy.

When we refuse to live our lives as an expression of agape love, we become like that unfortunate rock I tried to use as a hammer. Instead of serving our divine purpose, we get beat up by pouring our time and energy into almost anything else. We search for a sense of identity and value in what we do rather than who we are and what we're giving to others.

Scripture is very clear: love is our highest calling. We are called to love this world around us.

Our generation has an identity crisis. Many people I coach tell me they just don't know who they are or what they're supposed to give their life to—and these are not just younger people trying to find their way. Many senior adults well into their seventies find themselves asking these questions as well. Depression and anxiety are at an all-time high, in an era when life is more convenient than ever. There is an obsession with self-discovery, but few seem to be discovering anything that is making a real difference for them and their community.

I'm convinced we have an identity crisis because we have a love crisis. We have no idea what love is, much less how to love authentically.

If mutual affection is connected to submission, then agape love is always synonymous with sacrifice—giving up our own preferences, desires, comforts, and rights for the sake of our brothers and sisters. We give up what is important to us for the sake of the relationship. This is what this entire journey of enhancing our faith has been preparing us for—to love and sacrifice for others.

Whom Should We Love?

Though it is not always easy to love and make sacrifices even for those closest to us, God gifts and calls us to do just that for everyone. However, we tend to find it easier to love those who are lovable (usually those who are like us). Luke 6:32–33 tells us to take it a step further:

> *If you love those who love you, what credit is that to you? Even sinners love those who love them. And if you do good to those who are good to you, what credit is that to you? Even sinners do that.*

If we are to be agape love for each other, then we must sacrifice indiscriminately. How often do we withhold our love when people don't act the exact way we prefer? Do we choose to mitigate and reserve our love when others don't return our love in the manner we expect? Do we allow our theology to dictate?

When feelings are driving our love, we will inevitably love poorly. If we are going to live our purpose of expressing and expanding agape love to everyone we encounter, then we need a God who *is* love to continually fuel us.

It is impossible to say that we love God but not that person over there. And I'm sure we all have good reasons as to why "that person" or "that group" doesn't deserve full, sacrificial love. You may have piles of evidence built up over time to prove your point.

The fact is, the people you consider to be undeserving also carry divine spiritual DNA, a reflection of the Creator Himself. If we want to know how much we love God, all we need to do is look at how much we love our enemies. What if the only love that God experienced from you was the love you show to the person you care for the least? God sees the love we have for the people we'd rather not be around—yet God offered a sacrifice just as much for them as He did for us.

Serving a Sacrificial God

We are connected to a God who is exponentially more sacrificial than we could ever be—who has given more than we could ever consider giving back to Him—yet we creatively and consistently find ways of avoiding the sacrifices that we could make to and for Him.

How can we possibly serve a God who sacrifices more

than we do, out-giving us every time? No sacrifice could be greater than God giving His only Son out of love for a spiritually broken humanity.

The way we serve Him is to live a life of astounding, breathtaking and dynamic faith, trusting Him when He asks us to sacrifice back to Him. We serve Him by becoming like Him, joining in His mission to redeem all things through love.

Faith is intimately connected to the miraculous. My beautiful grandmother, MawMaw, says that faith is believing it is so, before it is so, so that it may be so. Our lives become evidence of the unseen things for which we hope.

Miracles always happen in the atmosphere of sacrifice. However, we often want an Exodus without having to deal with the slave master Pharaoh, and we want a glorious victory without facing Goliath. We want the glory of heaven without ever having to take up our cross.

We want better marriages, but we want our spouses to be the ones to change first. We want healthier finances, but we want to keep the lavish lifestyle that's draining our bank accounts. We want a deeper spirituality, but we don't want to give up our free time or resources to achieve that.

Everyone wants a miracle, but no one wants to sacrifice for it. When we are connected to Jesus, He will constantly call us into sacrificial love. And just when we think we have a handle on this sacrifice thing, He will call us into deeper levels of giving.

However, the call to a greater sacrifice is equally a call to a greater miracle.

If we are committed to living miraculous lives, we

must be committed to love. Part of my family's mission is to create atmospheres for the miraculous to occur, and we've surrendered to the reality that this means a life of consistent generosity in every aspect of living: relationally, spiritually, emotionally, mentally, physically, and financially. We must shake off the fear holding us back from making the sacrifice for love.

Love Casts Out Fear

I'm a coward by nature. I always admired my peers who exhibited natural self-assurance. As God calls me to take greater risks in my relationships, to give more of my resources, and as He calls the church I lead into deeper faith, I constantly find fear trying to take hold of me.

Fear is the enemy of love, seeking to strangle and kill love before it grows wings. Fear tells us that if we sacrifice, the natural result is that we will be left with less. We will find ourselves depleted, be let down, betrayed, hurt, overlooked, and disappointed. Fear stops us from loving fully.

The Bible assures us that perfect love—perfect sacrifice for the sake of another, empowered by God himself—will alleviate that fear:

> *There is no fear in love. But perfect love drives out fear, because fear has to do with punishment. The one who fears is not made perfect in love.*
>
> **—1 John 4:18**

Love creates a powerful context, a playground, for risk.

For example, when I am willing to sacrifice for my wife, it creates a safe place that invites her to thrive and take more risks in her life. She does the same for me. When we stop sacrificing for each other, the marriage breaks down and ceases to work. We lose our context for greater transformation.

Enhancing Our Mutual Affection with Love

Mutual affection calls us into suffering and love calls us into sacrifice. Talk about a combination that can cause anxiety and fear! We don't want to get hurt. We don't know what to expect. We don't even always know if our efforts are worth it immediately.

Some of us are praying for God to take away our anxiety before we commit to what He's asking of us. How many of us are completely willing to take a leap of faith *after* the risk factor is removed? God, however, tells us that once we start loving and sacrificing, we will find that fear's voice will be replaced with a far greater voice.

As we risk stepping out in faith for one another out of love, our capacity starts to expand in almost every area. Do you want greater influence? Start loving with the full power of God. Do you want greater responsibility? Start loving with the full power of God. Do you want greater passion? Start loving with the full power of God. Do you want an abundant life? Start loving with the full power of God.

Agape love is the antivenom to the soul-poison of fear. It's the highway to freedom and is never in short supply. If we want to have a fearless faith, we must supplement it with love. It's okay to start small, but start! As you are faithful with the little things, God will give you the greater things.

The list of enhancements prescribed in 2 Peter 1:5–7 is a journey we don't finish in a day. It's important to remember there is little *arriving* in the kingdom of God, but there is much *becoming*. It's about us becoming individuals and communities who can love fearlessly because we've been willing to fight through and persevere in this journey of faith.

And it is a fight. It's a fight not only for your freedom, but for the freedom of everyone else around you. A life infused with the unending love of God becomes an immovable agent of beauty in a world that is often so thrown to chaos. If we forsake the fight and forgo this journey, as many have, we will miss the glorious destination.

Love is worth it.

Chapter Seven Notes

CONCLUSION

Participating in the Divine Nature

God has given us the freedom to choose our path. Choosing Godlikeness is one of the greatest spiritual actions you will ever take. When we choose the journey to enhance our faith we find in 2 Peter, we become effective in living out the divine nature and purpose to which God has invited us.

> *For if you possess these qualities in increasing measure, they will keep you from being ineffective and unproductive in your knowledge of our Lord Jesus Christ.*
>
> ***—2 Peter 1:8***

Jesus is always leading us deeper into our faith journey, to give us more than we could ever ask or imagine. There is always more available to us. As we persevere in this journey, we will experience more love and hope for humanity, and find that we are living the story we were designed to tell.

This sacred journey will continue to enhance the faith

needed to continue to tell that story. Just as we enhance our physical bodies with supplements, these spiritual supplements will continually move us forward.

Here's the progression that we've followed throughout this book:

- *We enhance our faith with goodness*, meaning that we engage our faith from the perspective that God is good and He is working all things together for our good. Without this perspective, everything else falls apart.
- *We then enhance goodness with knowledge*, so that we can hold on to what we know to be true, even when our feelings tell us something different. Feelings are a dangerous and insufficient foundation for our faith. Knowledge keeps us steady.
- *We then enhance knowledge with self-control.* If knowledge is power, then we bear responsibility for the power we have been given. We are responsible for controlling our impulses and harnessing them for good.
- *We then enhance self-control with perseverance.* Anyone can be self-controlled for a moment, but perseverance must kick in when things become difficult. Self-control is doing the right thing repeatedly; perseverance is doing the right thing repeatedly when it's hard. It enables us to weather the storm and come out

on the other side.

- The next enhancement is *godliness*, which serves as the rudder of our ship and determines our destination when we persevere. Storms either elevate us or destroy us. Godliness determines whether we become bitter or more like God.
- God designed us as relational beings. Enhanced faith calls us to move outward into our relationships with others *with mutual affection*. This starts with submitting ourselves to each other and recognizing the oneness that Christ is working in and through us.
- Finally, *we enhance mutual affection with love*. Once we have chosen to submit to each other and pursue unity, we can allow sacrificial love to fill us, setting aside our preferences and rights for the sake of our brothers and sisters.

This powerful process is not about changing what we do, but changing who we are. It moves us from the corruption caused by our own destructive desires to a place where we can participate with our divine nature:

> *Through these he has given us his very great and precious promises, so that through them you may participate in the*

> *divine nature, having escaped the corruption in the world*

caused by evil desires.

—2 Peter 1:4

This implies that, just as with everything in life, we have a choice as to whether we participate in our divine nature. How we participate is our choice and determines our experience in this life, and the experience others have of us. We always participate in some way. The question is: what are we committed to? We may not be in the mood to participate fully, but we are not victims of our emotions.

Authenticity is not about being true to our feelings; it's acknowledging how we feel and then choosing to love anyway. Faith trumps emotion, enabling us to live in such a way that moves us to our divine nature.

We need faith to participate in life in a brand-new way, to believe that everything will be brilliantly new on the other side and that our best days are ahead of us. That is why Peter stresses the necessity of enhancing our faith. We will need a robust faith infused with love to live out the lives and create the environments that we were designed for.

The beautiful thing is that you *already* have been given everything you need to choose this journey right now. You are never without.

It's yours. What are you waiting for?

About the Author

Nathan Neighbour is a spiritual entrepreneur, speaker, coach, and transformational trainer who specializes in the arenas of spiritual development and character transformation. He began his professional career in the arts at age 12, working as on-air talent for the Children's Broadcasting Corporation—performing live with Disney, Universal Studios, and the Academy of Television and Radio. He continued his career in the performing arts, including work in theatre and music.

Nathan graduated from California Baptist University and holds a double master's degree in entrepreneur leadership and theological studies from Gateway Seminary. He spent seven years learning from and working with Mosaic LA, serving with the artisans and pastoral team. Nathan then founded Humanity Church in the heart of the arts colony in downtown Pomona. He currently serves as the lead pastor there, developing communities that speak to the core of human creativity and spirituality.

Nathan is also a certified transformational trainer and coach. He is passionate about seeing others experience freedom by realigning vision with commitment, discovering their uniqueness, and living out the dreams that are placed within their souls. Nathan strives to create spaces where communities become an intentional force of beauty, because he considers people's lives to be the most powerful medium to shape the future of humanity.

About Sermon To Book

SermonToBook.com began with a simple belief: that sermons should be touching lives, *not* collecting dust. That's why we turn sermons into high-quality books that are accessible to people all over the globe.

Turning your sermon series into a book exposes more people to God's Word, better equips you for counseling, accelerates future sermon prep, adds credibility to your ministry, and even helps make ends meet during tight times.

John 21:25 tells us that the world itself couldn't contain the books that would be written about the work of Jesus Christ. Our mission is to try anyway. Because in heaven, there will no longer be a need for sermons or books. Our time is now.

If God so leads you, we'd love to work with you on your sermon or sermon series.

Visit www.sermontobook.com to learn more.

REFERENCES

Notes

[1] "General Statistics: State by State." Insurance Institute for Highway Safety [and] Highway Loss Data Institute. https://www.iihs.org/iihs/topics/t/general-statistics/fatalityfacts/state-by-state-overview.

[2] McManus, Erwin Raphael. *The Artisan Soul: Crafting Your Life into a Work of Art*. Harper Collins, 2014. (I highly recommend all of this author's written work.)

[3] *The Best Exotic Marigold Hotel.* Directed by Dustin Hoffman. Blueprint Pictures, 2011.

[4] Strong, James. "G1108 – gnōsis." In *Strong's Exhaustive Concordance of the Bible* (Hunt & Eaton, 1894), quoted in Blue Letter Bible. https://www.blueletterbible.org/lang/lexicon/lexicon.cfm?t=kjv&strongs=g1108.

[5] Strong, "H337 – yir'ah," in *Strong's Exhaustive Concordance of the* Bible (Hunt & Eaton, 1894), quoted in

Blue Letter Bible. https://www.blueletterbible.org/lang/lexicon/lexicon.cfm?Strongs=H3374&t=KJV.

[6] McCall, David. "Schoolhouse Rock!" Theme song. Disney / ABC Domestic Television, 1973.

[7] Strong, "G5360 – "philadelphia," in *Strong's Exhaustive Concordance of the* Bible (Hunt & Eaton, 1894), quoted in Blue Letter Bible. https://www.blueletterbible.org/lang/lexicon/lexicon.cfm?Strongs=G5360&t=NIV.

[8] "Mutual." Lexico. https://www.lexico.com/en/definition/mutual.

[9] "Affection." Merriam-Webster. https://www.merriam-webster.com/dictionary/affection.

[10] Chapman, Gary. *The Five Love Languages: How to Express Heartfelt Commitment to Your Mate*. Northfield Publishing, 1995.

Made in the USA
San Bernardino, CA
10 March 2020

65532851R00071